FACE OF BRITAIN

Face of Britain

by Robin McKie

Foreword by Neil Oliver

Introduction by Sir Walter Bodmer

SIMON &
SCHUSTER

London • New York • Sydney • Toronto

First published in Great Britain by Simon & Schuster UK Ltd, 2006
A CBS company

3 5 7 9 10 8 6 4 2

Simon & Schuster UK Ltd
Africa House
64-78 Kingsway
London WC2B 6AH

www.simonsays.co.uk

Simon & Schuster Australia
Sydney

A CIP catalogue record for this book is available from the British Library

ISBN-10: 0743295293
ISBN-13: 9780743295291

Designed by Martin Lovelock
Additional maps by Peter Winfield
Printed and bound in Great Britain by CPI Bath

The Face of Britain TV series was produced by Wag TV for Channel 4
Director, Programmes 1 and 3: Martina Hall
Director, Programme 2: Helen Williamson and Jon Stephens
Graphic Designer: Keith Robinson
Executive Producers: Nick Godwin and Martin Durkin
Channel 4 Commissioning Editor: Hamish Mykura

Contents

Foreword

by Neil Oliver

T he population of Scotland in the first centuries after the last Ice Age would have fitted comfortably inside a double-decker bus. Or at least that's what I was told by the director of the first archaeological dig I worked on as a student. It was on a pre-historic site at a place called Loch Doon, in Ayrshire in 1985 and we were searching for flint tools, hut circles, and any other shadowy traces of the people who'd passed through the place 7,000 or 8,000 years before us. It sounds like an outrageous statement – and it will always be impossible to prove or disprove. But the sentiment behind it was reasonable enough: our earliest ancestors in these islands were few indeed.

In the years since, I've often imagined that bus-load of hunter-gatherers. It's certainly a vivid picture. But that they were so few in number, and lived and died as much as 10,000 years ago, always made them seem hopelessly ethereal to me; the most elusive of ghosts.

So when I got involved in *The Face of Britain* project, there was one claim that caught me hook, line and sinker: that the DNA from some of the passengers on that imaginary bus was still present within the cells of people living in Britain today. The coded messages that shaped the looks and personalities of those ancient forebears might still be shaping us today. All at once, the millennia separating me from those folk evaporated like mist. In many vital ways we still are those hunter-gatherers.

For a non-scientist like me, genetics is a mind-bogglingly complex subject. I read about the process of peering into the murky soup lying within our individual cells – a soup that somehow contains all of our potential to be who we are – and it's like looking into an abyss. It reminds me of the panic I knew so often at school when some or other science lesson began to get away from me.

In an attempt to grasp the underlying principles, I thought about my own family, my own bloodline, and where it might lead. And something simple struck me right away – it doesn't take many ancestors to get way back into the past. When I allowed 25 years for each generation, I realised that it took just 400 or so of them to get all the way back to those first hunters who came to Britain from Europe after the ice melted. And if you think of a lifetime lasting 70 years – three score and ten as the Bible has it – then just 150 lifetimes lived one after another reach right back 10,000 years or more. It really hasn't been so long after all.

And here in Robin McKie's account of the workings of this elegant project, something else that is simple and easily understood shines through. This is a story about people – some living today and some who lived out their lives uncounted centuries ago.

We humans are suckers for a good story well told. How astounding then to discover that each one of us carries a story within our own bodies? Each of us has within ourselves the story of who we are and who came before us. It's written in the language of DNA and it's floating silently within our cells, waiting to be read. Each of those individual stories is part of a greater whole, of course. Taken together, our collective DNA will eventually tell the story of mankind itself.

So, could there be a more fascinating project than that behind *The Face of Britain*? Samples taken from some thousands of volunteers will enable us to begin unravelling the threads of a fabric that has been thousands of years in the weaving. The individual strands will lead back – beyond recent immigrations, beyond the Norman Conquest; the coming of the Vikings; the Angles and Saxons; beyond the time of the Romans; beyond the Celts – all the way back to those folk who made these islands their home once the ice floes had retreated. In fact, it's a story that will one day lead all the way back to those long-lost bus passengers.

I like to think it's the start of the best story that we Britons will ever hear – the story of who we are and how we got here.

Introduction

by Sir Walter Bodmer

The People of the British Isles project, Oxford, England

We are all different, and in many ways: from our facial features, hair colour, and the size of our bodies, to our ways of moving and manner of speaking. This variation is one of the glories of the human species. There is a crucial exception to this rule, however, and that is provided by identical twins. They are often indistinguishable from each other – because they share an identical genetic make-up, an observation which tells us that most differences we use to recognise people are genetic in origin. Fortunately, the resulting profusion of different-looking people produced by these genetic variations is matched by our ability to recognise individuals.

Our unique appearances are also paralleled by our highly individual chemistries, such as our A, B and O blood types. These are determined by instructions written in the DNA molecules in our bodies' 100 million million cells, each of these being derived from a single fertilised egg created through the fusion of one sperm and one egg. An indication of how our chemistries vary is provided by studying the frequencies of those blood types among populations: type B is much more frequent in India than in England, for example. Thus a population can be characterised by a particular genetic signature. The more closely related the populations, the more similar their signatures. The people of Plymouth and Exeter have almost identical signatures, while these will be very different from those of Tokyo or Naples. The ability to characterise populations this way forms the basis for our project, The People of the British Isles.

The recent completion of the Human Genome Project means we now have an unprecedented amount of information about human genetic variation among populations – giving us greater power not just to study their genetic signatures but to investigate the inherited components of illnesses such as cancer, heart disease and mental illness. Such studies depend on a knowledge of the genetic history of populations – hence the Wellcome Trust's support for our project. Consider ankylosing spondylitis in which the backbone's vertebrae fuse together leading to a stiffened spine. It has been found that B27, one of the many genetically determined tissue types that are the basis of matching for transplantation, occurs in nearly everyone with the disease while less than 10 per cent of the population has type B27 tissue. This is a clear indication that B27 is involved in causing ankylosing spondylitis.

The results from such studies are not always clear cut, however. If a population is a mixture of peoples with two different genetic signatures, problems can arise. Consider multiple sclerosis. It occurs more frequently in Orkney than most areas of Britain. Orcadians have a mixture of Celtic and Viking ancestry so let us suppose multiple sclerosis susceptibility came with the Vikings. Knowing which piece of DNA was responsible for this effect would provide us with a key clue to the cause of the disease. However, we can only do that when we have learned to differentiate the differing genetic signatures of the Celtic and the Viking components of Orkney's population. This type of investigation is exactly what our study is about and we are applying it to the entire British Isles.

We are collecting blood samples from 100 to 150 individuals from each of about 30 rural locations around the country. However, only people whose four grandparents came from the same area are accepted. In this way we are maximising the chance of finding people whose ancestry can be traced back possibly to the earliest settlers to these areas, as well as their Roman, Anglo-Saxon, Viking and Norman successors. It should be noted, however, that people can have a profound cultural impact without having a major genetic influence. Consider the Romans. They had a huge influence on the organisation of life in England but because they used foreign garrisons to run the country, they almost certainly left few of their genes behind. It should also be stressed that the genetic differences between our populations are very slight. The differences between British Celts, Anglo-Saxons, Vikings and Normans arose by chance out of the early populations that migrated into Northern Europe after the last ice age. The sparsely distributed and relatively isolated populations of those times, 10,000 years ago, provided a good opportunity for the generation of genetic divergence. These differences may not be large but they are enough to distinguish the origins of the different groups who formed the people of the British Isles.

There is one obvious gap in our study, however. We have not taken account of recent waves of immigrants, including myself, a refugee from Nazi Germany. Though many have come, they still represent only a small proportion of the overall British population. In any case, their history relates to their country of origin, not to the British Isles. There are high concentrations of ethnic minorities in inner city areas, of course. Even in the distant past, most immigrants headed there to ply their trades. Hence our project's concentration on the rural population of the British Isles. On the other hand, Britain's population is certainly becoming more and more mixed up. My mother-in law, though well educated and from a middle class family, only travelled to London a few times in her life. That would be almost unimaginable nowadays. Clearly, the possibility of doing our project is rapidly diminishing. The traces of the origins of the people of the British Isles will very soon be lost for ever. Hence the urgency of our work.

Timeline

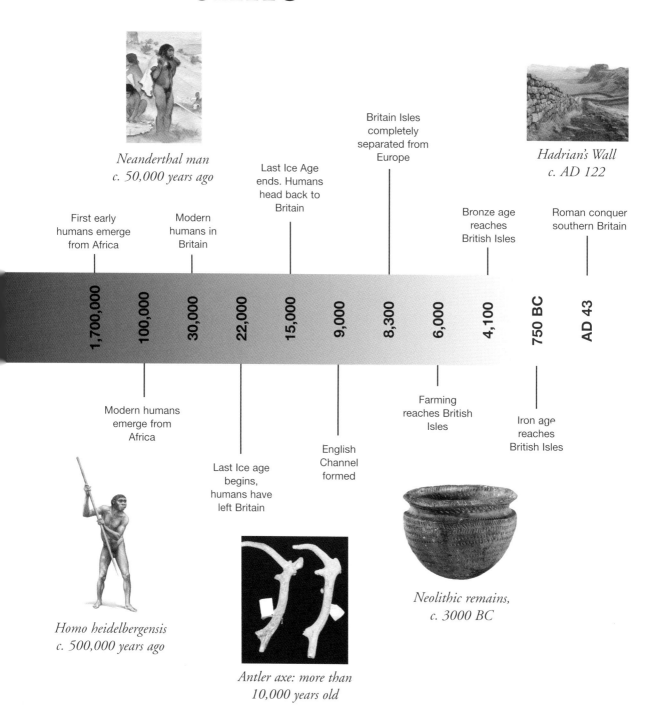

Neanderthal man
c. 50,000 years ago

Britain Isles
completely
separated from
Europe

Hadrian's Wall
c. AD 122

Last Ice Age
ends. Humans
head back to
Britain

First early
humans emerge
from Africa

Modern
humans in
Britain

Bronze age
reaches
British Isles

Roman conquer
southern Britain

1,700,000

100,000

30,000

22,000

15,000

9,000

8,300

6,000

4,100

750 BC

AD 43

Modern humans
emerge from
Africa

Last Ice age
begins,
humans have
left Britain

English
Channel
formed

Farming
reaches British
Isles

Iron age
reaches
British Isles

Homo heidelbergensis
c. 500,000 years ago

Antler axe: more than
10,000 years old

Neolithic remains,
c. 3000 BC

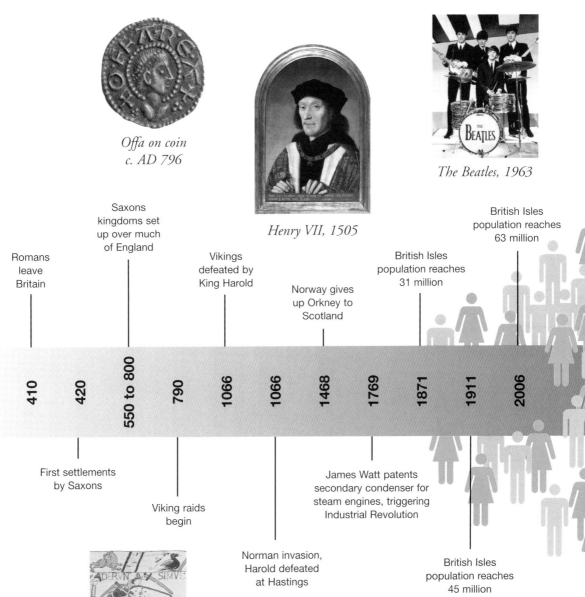

Offa on coin
c. AD 796

Henry VII, 1505

The Beatles, 1963

Romans
leave
Britain

Saxons
kingdoms set
up over much
of England

Vikings
defeated by
King Harold

Norway gives
up Orkney to
Scotland

British Isles
population reaches
31 million

British Isles
population reaches
63 million

410 **420** **550 to 800** **790** **1066** **1066** **1468** **1769** **1871** **1911** **2006**

First settlements
by Saxons

Viking raids
begin

Norman invasion,
Harold defeated
at Hastings

James Watt patents
secondary condenser for
steam engines, triggering
Industrial Revolution

British Isles
population reaches
45 million

Bayeux Tapestry
c. 1070

Lewis chessmen
c. 1150

William Shakespeare
c. 1625

Anno 1505 20 octobz imago henrich vii britanniæ regie illustrissimi
ordinata p hermann zinck to regie . . . . illorum . . .

CHAPTER ONE

Blood Count

I didn't know he was dead; I thought he was British.

WOODY ALLEN

When people say England, they sometimes mean Great Britain, sometimes the United Kingdom, sometimes the British Isles – but never England.

GEORGE MIKES, HOW TO BE AN ALIEN

At the top of the staircase that leads from the entrance hall of London's National Portrait Gallery into the heart of its display rooms, there is a small lobby devoted to Tudor monarchs. The gallery's earliest paintings are hung here in Room One, works that are surprisingly rich, colourful and free of the stylistic conventions that afflicted portraits of later centuries. There is a huge canvas devoted to Sir Thomas More and his family; several large portraits of the ever-corpulent Henry VIII; and a series of superbly painted images of court officials who stare disdainfully down at the crowds thronging the gallery. It is an intriguing set of faces, and nicely encapsulates the era, though the most important painting on display is, by comparison, a rather modest affair. It hangs just at the room's entrance and is often overlooked by visitors. This oil-on-panel portrait, a mere eighteen by twelve inches, depicts a slightly edgy-looking man holding a red rose in his right hand and who appears to be drumming impatiently with the fingers of his left, as if anxious to end the tedium of posing. You are looking at Henry VII and

A portrait of Henry VII, one of the earliest authenticated faces of Britain

the painting, dated 29 October 1505, is the oldest authenticated image of an individual in the National Portrait Gallery. This is the first face of Britain, if you like.

You can see older British 'portraits', of course. In another part of the gallery, there is a display containing a coin, smaller than a 1p piece and dated AD 796, with the head of Offa, King of Mercia, on it. This is the earliest face of an identifiable English ruler, according to gallery officials. But apart from Offa's strange bouffant hairstyle and his long, straight nose, it is impossible to make out any of his features, which is scarcely surprising given that his 'likeness' has been stamped on a piece of metal half an inch in diameter. It could just as easily be the image of a woman, quite frankly.

There are many other images of faces to be found in other parts of Britain, of course: on Iron Age and Roman coins, for example; on those great figures carved in the chalk hillsides of the downs of England, such as the Cerne Abbas giant in Dorset; and in a remarkable set of 2,600-year-old figurines, carved in wood, with pebble eyes (not to mention wooden penises that swivel), that were found at Roos Carr, in East Yorkshire and which are now displayed in Hull and East Riding Museum. However, according to UK archaeologist and Stone Age art expert Paul Bahn, the prize for old age should go to the rather contorted likeness of a man, carved on a woolly rhinoceros rib-bone, found in Pin Hole Cave, in Derbyshire, which is probably more than 14,000 years old.

Offa's image on a coin dating from AD 796

These figures demonstrate, if nothing else, an ancient fascination with the human face. None could be classed as portraits, however. Apart from their lack of finesse, these renditions could never be used to pinpoint an individual or to identify a person. Their purpose is largely symbolic. By contrast, that painting in Room One of the National Portrait Gallery is an authenticated likeness of a specific person. Henry's image is vivid, colourful, and has been expertly executed by an artist whose identity has unfortunately been lost over the centuries. Five hundred years on, the king – who had won the crown after defeating 'the bloody dog' Richard III, the last Plantagenet king of England, at Bosworth Field in 1485 – stares rather slyly at his audience, although his image was not meant for public gaze. It was painted as a part of an unsuccessful attempt by Henry to win the hand of Margaret of Savoy, daughter of the Holy Roman Emperor Maximilian I. (Henry's first wife, Elizabeth of York, bore him seven children, including Henry VIII. The last child was Katherine Tudor who died 2 February 1503. Nine days later, Elizabeth succumbed to a fatal post-pregnancy infection. It was her thirty-seventh birthday.) The royal suitor is shown here to have thin lips and a long, aquiline nose. His eyes are dark, his complexion slightly swarthy and his black hair is just beginning to show signs of grey. He looks Welsh, which is scarcely

The Cerne Abbas Giant in Dorset. The chalk figure's age is disputed

surprising given that Henry was born in Pembrokeshire. We should not make too much of this ancestry, however, for the background of Henry Tudor was complex. Suffice to say the painting is of a person who looks quintessentially British.

And that is why this portrait is so important to our story. It is a picture of a distinct and identifiable human being and a very British-looking one as well. Apart from his dodgy clothes, Henry would not have appeared out of place in the streets of Tunbridge Wells or Chelmsford today. Equally, you would have had no difficulty distinguishing him from other people in shopping malls and high streets. Henry's individuality is striking but then that is true for any Briton. To walk down a high street today is to be assailed by the sight of a parade of men and women who are short, tall, fat, thin, red-haired, curly-haired, bald, snub-nosed, green-eyed, big-chinned, barrel-chested, thick-set, or just plain ugly. The striking phenomenon is the variety of looks on display. It is a very useful feature, of course, for it makes it easy to work out one person from the next.

Much of this distinctiveness arises through individual differences that separate the people of any country, race or tribe. On the other hand, it is also possible to detect broad categories of appearances among the individuals that throng our supermarkets and stores. Some are swarthy like Henry, others are red and freckly, and some are blond and blue-eyed. But why? How can we explain the creation of these types? It is a fair set of questions and most of us would have no hesitation in answering them in terms of place. We would point to regions round the country where such appearances are reckoned to be common. Ginger hair and freckles suggest an origin in Scotland, for example. Those of a dark complexion are traditionally thought of as being Welsh in background. Geordies are said to have distinctive, high cheekbones.

And in adopting such regionalist urges, we follow a deep tradition. Visitors to this country have, through the ages, made a point of commenting on the variety of types of inhabitants from the islands' various parts. For example, the Roman historian Tacitus – whose father-in-law was Agricola, governor of the Roman province of Britannia – noted 'the reddish hair of the people who inhabit Caledonia [Scotland]' while also observing 'the swarthy faces of the Silures [a tribe from Wales], their generally curly hair'. He also commented on the similarities between south-east Englanders and the people of Gaul which he said were 'either due to continuing effects of heredity, or, where the lands jut out opposite one another, the climatic gave shape to the inhabitants' bodies'. In other words, there is a long history of viewing Britain as a mongrel nation.

But is there any rational underpinning to such observations? Have we any basis for believing the peoples of the different regions of the British Isles are intrinsically different from each other? Is there something in the blood that we can detect that allows us to differentiate the Scot from the Devonian and the Geordie from the Cumbrian? Until recently, the answer to these questions would have been a simple no. There was no effective way of teasing out such delicate biological information. Despite the tremendous advances that have taken place in biology over the past fifty years, many of them the work of UK scientists, little progress has been made in unravelling the genetic roots of the British people – until now. In the past few years, a number of key projects have been launched with the aim of tackling this issue and are already making dramatic progress. Of these, the largest and most ambitious is the People of the British Isles project, set up by the Oxford geneticist Sir Walter Bodmer.

This massive programme has been backed by a £2-million grant from the Wellcome Trust and has involved collecting blood from thousands of

British men and women, from Orkney to Kent, from Cornwall to Norfolk. These samples are being studied for their genetic content. By probing tiny discrepancies between genes in these samples, scientists are creating population maps of startling precision for the British Isles. One of the key aims of this ambitious undertaking is to help medical research and the search for the causes of common diseases, including cancers and other disorders. People vary in their susceptibility to disease because their genes are slightly different from those of other individuals. This may make it more likely that one individual will contract a particular illness than another person. So by working out different patterns of variations of different genes, and different combinations of genes, and by matching these with distributions of diseases, it may be possible to unravel some of

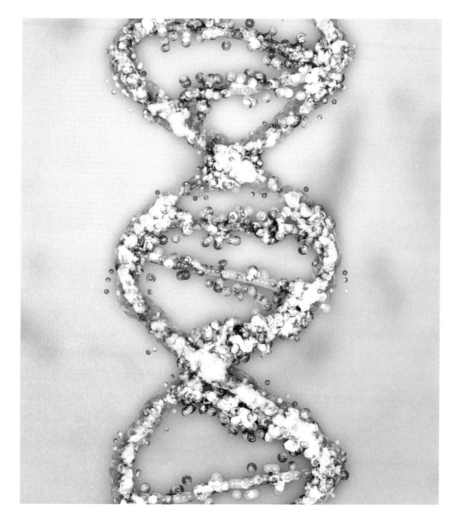

Strands of DNA forming a double helix

the causes of these various conditions. It was with this entirely laudable goal that the People of the British Isles project was launched.

But if medicine was the prime motivating factor for the setting up of the project, history and archaeology also stand to gain from this grand-scale bleeding of the British people. The maps that Bodmer will create will not only tell us about our proneness to illness, they will give vital clues to the movements of our ancestors, the men and women who established these bloodlines in the first place. 'Ultimately, we will look at about 3,000 genetic variations in our subjects,' says Bodmer. 'We can already see how common some genetic variants are in certain areas while others are infrequent. It is allowing us to establish the key influences involved in the shaping of the British people.'

Some of the variants involve blood types, others are concerned with hair colour, and a few with the behaviour of our immune systems. Fluctuations of different versions of these genes, across the country, provide perfect clues about past population movements. And in these patterns of distribution, scientists can already discern the ancient biological footprints of the Anglo-Saxons, the Vikings and the very first people who settled in Britain when it was still linked by land to the continent and was just recovering from the impact of the last Ice Age. The roots of the British people may be deeply buried but they are at last giving up their secrets.

This, then, is the story of the face of Britain. In this book we shall explore the underlying causes of the diversity of the men, women and children who make up the population of the British Isles today. It is not an account of the intricacies of human genetics – although the subject is undoubtedly fascinating. Detailed biological explanations have been kept to a minimum. However, for those wishing to delve a little deeper into the science and technology of this intriguing detective story, there is an appendix which covers not only the techniques employed by geneticists but many of the tools employed by archaeologists and historians.

Equally, this is not a history book. Although roughly structured in chronological order, subjects have been selected because of their influence on the make-up of the British people, not because they are considered important to scholars. Some incomers – like the Romans – had little effect on our bloodline and so are accorded relatively little space. Others

– like the Anglo-Saxons – had a significant impact, and receive a great deal of attention as a result. In addition, those seeking detailed scrutiny of the movements of the various tribes around Britain will also be disappointed. I have deliberately avoided such issues, in the main to avoid the type of historical confusion that was so gloriously lampooned by W.C. Sellar and R.J. Yeatman in *1066 and All That* as they wrote: 'The Scots (originally Irish, but by now Scotch) were at the time inhabiting Ireland, having driven the Irish (Picts) out of Scotland; while the Picts (originally Scots) were now Irish (living in brackets) and vice versa. It is essential to keep these distinctions clearly in mind.' You get the point.

It is also worth mentioning, briefly, the issue of nationality. This book is about the people of the British Isles and is therefore concerned not just with the Scots, Welsh and English of mainland Britain but the inhabitants of Ireland, both north and south, and the rest of the British archipelago, including the Isle of Man, the Hebrides and the island groups of Orkney and Shetland. As we shall see, modern science can now detect connections between these people, links that often defy modern borders. We have attempted at all times to label these different nationalities as precisely as possible and to avoid upsetting sensibilities. (As a Scot, I find it irritating – but only mildly – to be addressed as an Englishman, usually by Americans, so I have tried to tread with care.) Doubtless, I have stumbled on occasions, and apologise in advance.

I should also make it clear at this point that this book will not be concerned with an issue that is one of the most welcome and invigorating aspects of modern British life: the nation's increasing ethnic mix. When I look at the faces in my children's classroom photographs, I see British faces that clearly show their friends have genetic histories which lie in Africa, the Caribbean, the Indian subcontinent, China and South East Asia. These backgrounds are every bit as important as those outlined in this book but they are also recent and relatively easy to elucidate. Our prime concern in *The Face of Britain* is to show how scientists are teasing out a much more mysterious genetic inheritance that goes back to the beginnings of recorded history and into the depths of our prehistoric past.

The Face of Britain shows how science is linking people with the settlers who first came to this land thousands of years ago. From these connections we will explain the roots of many of the variations that exist

Francis Crick and James Watson in 1953

across the British Isles and indicate how they point to the way land was used and occupied. Thus the following chapters will show why Scotland has so many redheads and suggest that this effect was not necessarily just the result of a throw of the genetic dice. Having red hair may be evolutionary good sense. We will also reveal the traces that demonstrate people's Viking roots. We will meet some of the individuals who have provided the blood samples upon which these projects are based and hear how their tales throw a vivid light on their past and our history. We will hear about one of the most striking discoveries to have been made in the field in the past few years: that most of the genes of the British people today can be traced to the very first people who settled on the land more than 12,000 years ago. We may have some Viking blood or Anglo-Saxon genes or hail from a Norman family, but, deep under our skin, the majority of the British population are really Stone Age hunter-gatherers.

Teasing out these subtle signs from our past has been anything but easy. In fact, it has been an extremely awkward and elusive task, thanks – in the main – to the basic biology of *Homo sapiens*. Members of our species differ from each other because of variations in our genes, the basic units of inheritance, which are made of a substance called deoxyribonucleic acid, DNA, a magical molecule that lies coiled in the nucleus at the centre of each cell in our bodies. The way in which scientists worked out the structure of DNA – which turns out to be a double helix – is one of the most exciting stories of discovery ever told and rightly brought fame and a Nobel prize to the two brash young Cambridge researchers who were responsible: James Watson and Francis Crick. Most of the discoveries revealed in this book are a direct consequence of the success of their scientific sleuthing in 1953. The critical factor is that DNA controls the production of proteins, the building blocks of our bodies. Slight changes between one person's DNA and another's are responsible for producing those subtle variations in eye, hair and skin colour, physique and height that differentiate each of us from the rest of humanity.

It all sounds straightforward. The trouble is that these changes are very slight indeed, for the mechanisms that direct the construction of the proteins that define us are controlled by only tiny amounts of DNA. Every human being on Earth has 3 billion units of DNA and all of us share 99.9 per cent of that DNA. In other words, of the 3 billion units of DNA, 2.997 billion are also possessed by your next-door neighbour, your boss, your MP, your bank manager, Wayne Rooney, the royal family, and every person on the planet. Variations in that remainder, that 0.1 per cent of our DNA, are therefore responsible for all the differences that separate each member of our species from every other member, and, it should be added, that covers not just the issue of appearance. Other attributes that define individuals – intelligence, personality, artistic ability, scientific genius, and a great deal more – arise from those slight DNA changes. Thus only tiny alterations in each of our double helices produce an entire planet of highly variable human beings. This is one of the oddest aspects of our species. Consider our nearest evolutionary neighbours. Researchers have found there is more genetic diversity in a single group of chimpanzees than there is in the human population of the world. As David Woodruff of the University of California, San Diego, puts it: 'From a chimpanzee's point of view, we all look like Dolly the Sheep.' In other words, we are virtually clones of each other so similar is our DNA. Thus when we look at those red-haired, blue-eyed individuals with high foreheads who throng our shopping malls and bars, you should remember that only a few delicate variations in their genes were required to produce this hotchpotch of humanity. So the next time you are in the National Portrait Gallery, after taking a good look at Henry in Room One, wander through the rest of the collection of politicians, scientists, artists, actors, sportsmen and women, kings and queens, servants, soldiers and inventors. All these images are of people who were produced by only slender switches in DNA. As a species, and as a people, we have made very little go a very long way.

Now two key issues spring from this appreciation of our tight genetic affinity with each other. The first is a practical one. If the roots of our physical variation are based on such slight genetic differences, and are buried like genetic needles in haystacks of DNA, they will not reveal themselves with ease. This is certainly true. It has taken considerable ingenuity on the part of scientists to work out how to expose these tiny alterations. We will encounter some of the key technologies involved in this unravelling in later chapters and show how important they have been in revealing the lineages of the people of the British Isles.

The second issue raised by scientists' discovery of our close genetic similarity with each other is even more important – for it has immediate relevance to the arrival of men and women on the shores of the British Isles. It turns out that *Homo sapiens* is genetically closely knit for a very simple reason: it is an incredibly young species, one that evolved from a small core of founding males and females a mere 150,000 to 200,000 years ago somewhere south of the Sahara. Not long afterwards, around 100,000 years ago we emerged from our African cradle and took over the world. In terms of the natural selection of creatures on this planet this was a mere blink of an eye, a brief existence that implies we have not had time to evolve major genetic differences from one another. Indeed, the issue may go even further than this. Geneticists have found out that not long before our African emergence, there had been a population crash among our ancestors that would have reduced their numbers to about 10,000 individuals. At that time, we would have been clinging on desperately to only a small stretch of African territory and would have been far too thinly spread to move into new lands. The rest of the world would have been left to other species while we would have been as endangered as orang-utans and mountain gorillas today. But we survived this population bottleneck and in the end flourished to the extent that our numbers have grown until there are now six and a half billion of us on the planet. Yet all are the creation of a group of individuals, drastically reduced in numbers, who thrived a few tens of millennia ago. We should therefore not be surprised by our tight genetic heritage.

We should also note at this stage that we were not the first human beings to make it out of Africa. We were beaten to the tape almost two million years ago by *Homo erectus*, one of the ancestor species of modern humans. They too walked away from their African homeland and began to settle in different corners of the globe. Fossils, dated as being

1.7 million years old, have been discovered in Georgia, near Tbilisi, while other ancient erectus finds have been made in Indonesia. More importantly for our story, we now know that one line of these ancient humans eventually made it to Europe: one set of ancient bones have been found at Gran Dolina in Spain and dated as being around 800,000 years old, for example. Then about half-a-million years ago, these ancient men and women reached Britain. It was a lineage doomed to extinction, however. Indeed, it is one of the most uncomfortable facts about our evolution that when modern humans arrived on the world scene 100,000 years ago, all other members of humanity, including the Neanderthals, were wiped out in a very short space of time. We became sole masters of

An artist's impression of a Neanderthal family

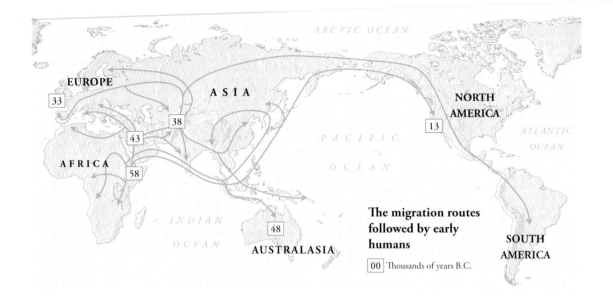

How the world was won: the spread of Homo sapiens *across the globe*

the planet with disturbing speed.

It is a striking success story, nevertheless. Thanks to their remarkable ability to adapt and plan, modern humans spread inexorably round the globe and with far greater rapidity and impact than their *Homo erectus* predecessors. First *Homo sapiens* moved into Asia, and then on to Australia. Later Europe succumbed, with the peninsula of Britain – then attached to the continent by a land bridge – being inhabited by around 30,000 years ago. Finally North and South America were occupied when *Homo sapiens* crossed from Asia to land that is now Alaska about 15,000 to 20,000 years ago. It was not a pell-mell rush for new lands, however. 'The movement was probably imperceptible,' says US geneticist Spencer Wells. 'It was less of a journey and probably more like walking a little further down the beach to get away from the crowd.' In the end, one set of those African beachcombers ended up on the shores of Britain and made their homes there. The surprising find has been to discover from our genes how little we have changed since their arrival.

But this is the power of genetics. It allows scientists to tackle a host of concerns about our species: our susceptibilities to different illness, the roots of our personalities, and the nature of our intellectual capabilities. But it can also reveal the secrets of our ancestors, for genes above all else are messengers from the past. They can tell us who possessed them and who nurtured them and ensured they were passed on to future generations. Indeed, genes can often tell us more about our history than traditional methods for investigating ancient events. Genes do not crumble in the ground or rust in the air. They are unaffected by the elements, as British anthropologist Jonathan Kingdon points out:

> Fossil bones and footsteps and ruined homes are the solid facts of history, but the surest hints, the most enduring signs, lie in those minuscule genes. For a moment we protect them with our lives, then like relay runners with a baton, we pass them on to be carried by descendants. There is a poetry in genetics which is more difficult to discern in broken bones, and genes are the only unbroken living thread that weaves back and forth through all those bone-yards.

This point is stressed by Neil Oliver. 'Genetics is another kind of archaeology,' he says. 'It deals with something that has been left inside of us. That makes it a very powerful technique.' It is a good point, for that is exactly what scientists are now exploiting. They are testing and investigating things inside us in order to tell the men and women of this archipelago about their history. Not that its people are likely to give up that information overnight. We are, after all, a complex, baffling, disparate bunch of individuals, a mongrel people whose royalty is really German, whose dress sense was created by Walloons and refined by Huguenots, whose banks were based on models established by the Dutch, whose most notable meal – the Sunday lunchtime roast – was imported by the Romans, and whose crown jewels were plundered from Asia and Africa.

It also must be acknowledged that in cultural terms, we are a very odd mixture: part Norman, Anglo-Saxon, colonial, Celtic and who knows what else. Now the People of the British Isles project is allowing us to find out how this complexity is matched by the make-up of our genes – which leads us to another important point. Culture – in the form of new ideas, processes, fashions, styles of pottery, methods of metal working and a host of other processes – can arrive in two ways: in the wake of an invading army or as a slow infusion of ideas from neighbouring lands and people. Until recently, it has proved to be extremely difficult to tell which of these two processes have been most involved in our history. As the archaeologist David Miles has pointed out: 'Just because you find a Coca-Cola can in a rubbish bin, doesn't mean a place has been invaded by Americans.' But now, thanks to geneticists, we are beginning to unravel the role of incomers and immigrants in our story and provide explanations for the arrival of new types of culture, like that of the Anglo-Saxons. Thus we are resolving, for the first time, a fundamental puzzle: was it people or ideas that determined the fate of the British Isles? Again, this topic will form a key component of this book.

Of course, much of the character of the British people rests on the fact that we live on an archipelago. Our isolation has meant that we have dealt with new experiences and ideas in our own way, a point summed up by the archaeologist Christopher Smith: 'It is characteristic of societies in large islands that have substantial populations isolated from other groups that they develop rather idiosyncratic responses to social, economic and technology issues.' This point is backed by the journalist and author Jeremy Paxman: 'The first profound influence upon the English is the fact that they live on an island.' And what is true for the English, is true for the rest of the group of islands.

We should not make too much of our isolation, however, as David Miles cautions:

There are times when the Channel has played the part of a moat, defended by the wooden walls of the fleet against Napoleon's giant armies, or by squadrons of Hurricanes and Spitfires. For more often though, the sea has acted as a highway linking Liverpool to Dublin and North America, Whitby to London and Australia, Kirkwall to Reykjavik or Oslo, Cork and Cornwall to Brittany. The outside world does not bounce off the White Cliffs of Dover; rather it washes around them and into the inlets of the Thames, Ouse, Humber and Trent, the Tyne, Forth, Clyde, Dee, Mersey, Severn and Shannon.

In this way, the sea has been a critical factor in the creation of the British people. It has protected us at times, and mastering it has allowed us to go on to conquer a large part of the world. We should not get too carried away with ourselves, however. Our partial isolation has also helped to create a population of considerable eccentricity, as the US travel writer and Anglophile Paul Theroux once observed. On overhearing a Briton dismissing Americans for their oddness, he erupted into a diatribe on the British character:

> They wallpaper their ceilings! They put little knitted bobble-hats on soft-boiled eggs to keep them warm! They say sorry when you step on their toes! Their government makes them get a hundred dollar licence every year for watching television. They drive on the left! They spy for the Russians! They call their houses Homeleigh and Sparrow View! They don't say 'you're welcome'! They still have milk bottles and milkmen and junk-dealers with horse-drawn wagons! They love candy and Lucozade and leftovers called bubble and squeak! They live in Barking and Dorking and Shellow Bowells! They have amazing names like Mr Eatwell and Lady Inkpen and Major Twaddle and Miss Tosh! And they think we are odd.

Viewed from this perspective we are a little unusual, it must be admitted, particularly as nearly all the items on this list of oddities – written by Theroux in his 1983 book *The Kingdom by the Sea*, his account of his journey round the coast of Britain, are still relevant today.

The remarkable variety (though not necessarily the oddness) of the people in the British Isles is, of course, the focus of this book. Much of the information we will discuss has revealed itself through the work of geneticists. However, other intriguing new sources have been developed. One of these is the study of names which – thanks to the use of huge computer databases – means it is now possible to trace the distribution of surnames across Britain over the past century and so pinpoint the origins of some of the most familiar names: Attenborough, Paxman and Rooney, for example. At the same time, scientists have developed techniques for putting faces to the ancient skulls that have been unearthed by archaeologists and so provide us with a glimpse of what an ancient Celt or an Anglo-Saxon might have looked like. In fact, the real surprise is that so many technologies are now reaching fruition and have given us the opportunity to reveal the true face of Britain for the first time.

CHAPTER TWO

Red Shift

*When red headed people are above a certain
social grade their hair is auburn.*

MARK TWAIN

There is a small, windowless room on the ground floor of Oxford's Radcliffe Infirmary that can be reached only by walking through a maze of narrow passageways. The hospital is old even by the normal standards of ageing National Health Service buildings in the UK. The Radcliffe was built in the late-eighteenth century and its corridors are narrow. There is little chance of seeing much of the outside world once you get down to this, the gloomiest part of the building. The hospital may have charm, but it is certainly not a glittering high-technology citadel.

Nevertheless, it is in these antiquated surroundings that scientists have set up one of the most ambitious biological programmes ever attempted in Britain. This is the base of the People of the British Isles project which is now using the power of modern genetics to show how people in different regions met and interacted over the past few thousand years, how they subjugated one another, and how they passed on ideas, inventions and art. The hub of this project, which is led by Walter Bodmer, rests in that little cubbyhole on the ground floor of the Radcliffe Infirmary.

There is a bench fitted with high-technology gear used to isolate and copy DNA; a couple of tables with personal computers; and – most important of all – several tall fridges around the room's bare walls.

A wonderful vision of red hair. 'Lady Lilith' by Charles Dante Rossetti

Unearthing Treasures

Ken Sweet, a retired architect's draughtsman, who lives in Polgooth, near St Austell in Cornwall, is typical of the donors recruited by Bodmer. His grandparents all lived nearby. Indeed, Sweet can trace his father's descendants back for sixteen generations to the area, to around 1530, while on his mother's side, he can reach back to around 1750. Sweet says:

I felt it was really important to take part in this project because I don't think it will be possible to carry out a programme like it in another decade. My family were Cornish through and through, but already things are changing. They have married people from outside Cornwall which would probably have seemed unthinkable in my grandparents' day. My children do not live that far away but their children may well end up moving to more distant locations one day. Society is becoming more and more mobile and house prices in Cornwall are so high that moving, for them, may be inevitable. When they go, the thread that has linked my family for centuries to this land will have been broken.

Sweet's ancestors were all tin miners and given the antiquity of the industry in south-west England, this suggests his lineage may be a very deep one indeed. Archaeologists have found evidence that tin was mined here thousands of years ago. For example, six pieces of tin slag – the waste from tin smelting – were found underneath a Bronze Age barrow at nearby Caeloggas. And by the time the Romans reached Britain, tin mining was a major industry with traders shipping the stuff off to Spain, Brittany, Ireland and Wales. Sweet, who is now seventy-three, is proud but not sentimental about these connections:

*Cornish tin miners
at Redruth Mine
in the 1920s*

My grandfather had six brothers. Of the seven, four – including my
grandfather – went to work at Great Polgooth tin mine. He died
aged thirty-eight and he was the oldest survivor of the four miner
brothers. You were lucky to live much beyond thirty if you were a
tin miner. The dust in the mine caused a wasting disease of the
lungs called phthisis. The trouble was, there was little else you could
do to make a living. Essentially, you married young, had your family
young and then you died young.

Given this grim history, and the strong likelihood of an early death,
it is all the more remarkable that a dynasty of Sweets now flourishes
around Polgooth. Their genealogical thread could have been easily
cut at any time, a fate that must have befallen hundreds of
thousands of others over the millennia. 'I am just glad we have a
chance to get another look at how our ancestors got here, and how
the Cornish people came to be here in the first place,' says Sweet.
He had answered an advert placed by Bodmer and his team in local
papers for donors. About fifty people turned up at the 'blooding' –
set up at an Exeter hospital – for the Cornish part of the project.
Sweet was one of them. 'We have had no shortage of volunteers,'
Bodmer admits. 'People are fascinated by their ancestors and the
thought that they might be helping to uncover new facts and ideas
has proved to be irresistible.'

Open one and you will see rows of vials, as you would in most laboratories. These containers are special, however, for they hold the bloodline of the British people. Each vial contains DNA from a person who has taken part in Bodmer's project and each sample has its own special story to tell. 'Every drop of human blood contains a history book written in the language of the genes,' the US geneticist Spencer Wells once remarked. It is a good description. So think of these vials, not as containers of chemicals, but as books, and view those fridges, not as storage facilities, but as bookcases in a library devoted to the history of the British and Irish people.

Of course, fresh volumes have to be obtained to maintain any great reference collection, which in this case means getting plentiful supplies of blood from the public. The whole purpose of the project is to sample as widely as possible in order to uncover the maximum amount of information. Bodmer says: 'We have a strict policy about donors. We stick to rural areas because urban populations are already far too mixed up for us to be to able to tease out their genetic roots. In the countryside there has been much less genetic input from "outsiders" over the past century. People there give us a far better picture of ancient population patterns.'

Rural residency on its own is insufficient for inclusion in the project, however. A volunteer's two parents, and all four grandparents, also have to come from the same area. 'A century ago, public transport – mainly trains – had not had a major effect in shaking up the population,' states Bodmer. 'We are after all the descendants of people who have deep roots in a particular area and by selecting not just them, but their grandparents, that will help us to get to their ancestors.'

A total of eleven sites were selected for blood collections for the project's pilot study, the aim being to provide the maximum amount of information about past population movements, waves of immigrations, and invasions, from the minimum number of locations. Those chosen were: Orkney; north-east England; Cumbria; Lincolnshire; Norfolk; Suffolk; Oxfordshire; Pembrokeshire; Kent/Sussex; Devon; and Cornwall. (Further locations are scheduled to be added in future years.) Consider the example of Orkney. These islands can provide priceless data not just about the Scots but about Norse influences on the British Isles, one of the most fascinating aspects of our entire saga, as we shall see. Similarly Cornwall and Devon were rated promising hotspots for signs

Sites of blood collection

Orkney

North-East
England

Cumbria

Lincolnshire

Norfolk

Suffolk

Oxfordshire

Pembrokeshire

Kent &
Sussex

Devon &
Cornwall

ATLANTIC

OCEAN

North

Sea

Irish

Sea

English Channel

N

*Locations of blood
collection points for
the People of the
British Isles project*

that the descendants of the very first, most ancient people may live on in some areas while Kent and Suffolk were considered likely to provide most data about the impact of the Anglo-Saxons. In this way, the project's scientists hope to deduce a massive amount about the build-up and movement of people across the whole of the archipelago over the past 15,000 years.

As to the actual collecting of blood, this was simplified to make it as comfortable and straightforward as possible. It is a technique that has been developed over the years and is used for many types of blood screening. First, a volunteer's skin is pierced with a needle which is attached to a small tube, known as a Vacuette. Air has already been pumped from the tube, producing a vacuum that sucks blood out of the volunteer's vein, through the needle and into the Vacuette. This process is repeated using a second tube, creating two 9-millilitre blood samples. Inside the tubes, the blood mixes with a liquid anticoagulant to prevent it from clotting. Then the two Vacuettes – each volunteer's genetic contribution to the People of the British Isles project – are sent, by first-class post, to the Radcliffe Infirmary laboratory.

'All samples have to be posted the same day they are taken,' adds Bruce Winney, the project's manager. 'Nor are samples ever sent out on a Friday. They might not reach us until the Monday and by that time their white cells could start to decay and die.' This is a crucial point, for as we shall see, white cells are a vital source of information for unravelling human ancestry. Once a sample arrives at the centre, researchers open the tubes, put the blood in new containers and spin these on centrifuges for thirty minutes. 'This creates several layers made up of different blood components,' says Winney. 'Of these, there are only two that are of interest to us and these are the ones that have white cells in them. At the bottom of the centrifuge tube there is a crimson goo of red and white cells, and further up there is a cloudy layer that is made up mostly of other white cells.'

White cells are of prime interest because of their DNA. Our blood's other main component, its red cells, have no genetic machinery for replication. After carrying oxygen molecules around our arteries for a couple of months, red cells die out and are replaced by new ones manufactured in our bone marrow. However, white cells – which regulate and operate our immune defence systems – are stuffed with DNA. The two different layers containing white cells obtained from the centrifuge are dealt with in separate ways, however. First, the cloudy layer of white cells is cooled on blocks of dry ice, before being placed in tubes chilled to minus 190 degrees Celsius. These are then stored in freezers for possible use in future studies. 'This is the DNA we save for a rainy day,' says Winney. Ultimately, more than 3,500 samples like these will be collected by the time the project is completed in 2009.

The other part of the donor's sample – the crimson sludge at the bottom of the centrifuge – is treated straightaway by adding a chemical known as a lysing agent. This destroys the membranes that hold the cells together, causing them to split open. In the case of the white cells, their DNA then spills out. Finally, using a variety of different chemical treatments, the project technicians sweep away all the other cellular detritus in their tubes until they are left with pure DNA. Not that they get much for their efforts: at the end of the day about a tenth to half of a gram of the stuff is all that remains of each volunteer's blood sample.

Such portions would not go far given the ambitious schedule that Bodmer and his team have set for themselves. Only plentiful supplies of DNA could satisfy their ultimate plans for a total of 3,000 tests to be carried out on each donor's blood. These include tests to pinpoint a donor's blood group and rhesus factor and also the variants of the HLA system – or human leukocyte antigen system – that they possess. (The HLA system consists of biological markers that cover cells, acting as biochemical signatures, and are of crucial importance when matching tissue for transplants.) In addition, for men, their Y-chromosome variants will be studied. (The Y-chromosome confers masculinity and is handed down, intact, from father to son, through the generations – making it a very useful tool for tracking the movement of people.) In total, this is a considerable list. The geneticists have one handy ally, however: PCR – or DNA amplification. This technology has the capacity to make billion-fold copies of particular stretches of genetic material. This has allowed tell-tale sections of DNA from bones of ancient Britons to be multiplied a billion

A scientist working on the People of the British Isles project checks donors' blood samples

times and to reveal the secrets of our ancestors, as we shall see in the next chapter. It has also helped many other scientists tease out data from flimsy scraps of genetic material.

To create their PCR copies, the project's technicians place each donor's DNA into a tube into which are added special chemicals known as oligonucleotides. These isolate sections of the donor's DNA at precise points, so that when the PCR machine is switched on, these sections and only these sections will be copied a billion-fold. Only certain gene variants will be multiplied this way, however. By carefully selecting their oligonucleotides, the project scientists can pinpoint precise pieces of DNA for copying. In other words, they can snip out the gene variant they are seeking from a donor's DNA and then create copies of it. If that variant is not in a sample, no copies will be made, of course. 'We often look for a couple of variants in a particular section of DNA, ones that will hopefully tell us something about the prehistory of the British people,' Bodmer says. 'If they are present in a person's blood, the oligonucleotides will latch on to them and the PCR will grow them up. But if the variants are not in the donor's DNA, then the oligonucleotides will have nothing to latch on to, and the DNA will not grow up.'

All the scientists have to do then is find a way to detect if DNA has been multiplied or not. This is done by adding special fluorescent dyes that adhere only to DNA. If a piece of DNA has been grown up a billion times it will glow strongly when illuminated by light beams. If it was not present in the original sample, no copies will have been made and there will be no glow from the sample. 'When that happens, we get a nil result which is just as interesting as a positive result,' adds Bodmer. In this way, he and his team began to build up a pattern of different genetic variants for different parts of the British Isles, and from the moment they started to pull data from their machines, and keyed them into their computers, their findings produced surprises.

Consider the project's very first results. These focused on two variants of a gene called the melanocortin 1 receptor, or MC1R. It is not a very exciting name but it is an important one for our story, for the two variants of this gene are responsible for one of the most conspicuous aspects of the British and Irish population: our redheads. Whether they are called carrot-tops, ginger-heads, or 'Titian blondes', these people are blessed –

or cursed, according to some of them – with flaming locks that have been a feature of British and Irish people for millennia, from Boudicca to Churchill. The underlying causes of the condition were recently disentangled by a team led by Professor Jonathan Rees, a dermatologist based at Edinburgh University. It discovered that hair colour is controlled by the MC1R gene, which is found on chromosome number 16. As we have noted, genes come in different variants and there are about seventy different versions of this gene. Rees discovered that a subgroup of about half a dozen of these is closely involved in determining if a person will be red-haired or not. 'If you have one of these variants, your chances of having red hair are increased four or five times above the average,' says Rees. 'However, if you have two of these variants – one inherited from your mother, and one inherited from your father – your chances of being red-haired increase to thirty to forty times the average. Equally, if you have neither variant, and possess a couple of different gene versions, it is highly unlikely you will have red hair.' (The combination of two 'red-hair' variants of the MC1R gene is now exploited by forensic scientists when testing blood left behind at crime scenes. If they find both variants present in a sample, police know there is a strong chance the culprit will be a redhead.)

Red hair today is generally associated with the Scots and Irish though there have been no consistent efforts to establish the prevalence of the condition over the decades. Nor have matters improved. 'It has actually become harder to find the prevalence of red hair today,' adds Rees. 'More and more women – and some men – now dye their hair and we simply have no idea if a red head is a real one or if a blonde is a red head under the dye. As a result the incidence of red hair in Britain is still a bit of a mystery.'

Or at least it was. Thanks to Bodmer and his team, this most distinctive characteristic is now opening up its mysteries for the first time. In selecting tests for his surveys, Bodmer picked ones that would pinpoint two of the half-dozen versions of the MC1R gene that are responsible for red hair. (These are known as the R151C and the R160W variants.) Oligonucleotides that latch on, specifically, to these variants were added to the donor's DNA. And it is worth noting here that one gene variant differs from another by only the tiniest chemical change. A gene is typically made up of several tens of thousands of base pairs. However, it takes only one alteration to one of these base pairs (these single changes are called 'single nucleotide polymorphisms' or 'snips' by scientists) to produce a complete transformation in the gene's behaviour in the body, causing it to help to make red pigment in hair or to block its production. The startling precision with which molecular biologists can latch on to these minute alterations has been critical to the success of Bodmer's project.

Bodmer and his team then began hunting for their variants. Each time they got a positive result from their PCR analysis of their blood samples, they noted it in their records. Each time they got a negative one, they recorded this as well. In this way, the prevalence of these two pieces of DNA were collated for each area of the British Isles. These figures were then expressed as a frequency for that region. One is the maximum possible value. The results were intriguing. In Cornwall and Devon, Bodmer got figures of 0.16 and 0.23 for the frequencies of red-hair genes, while in Wales the figure was 0.21, and in Orkney 0.26. This last figure is high, particularly when compared with other areas. The frequency for red-hair genes in Oxfordshire was 0.07; in Sussex and Kent 0.13; in north-east England 0.11; in Lincolnshire 0.07; and – most striking of all – in Cumbria, it was nil. (It should be noted these figures represent the frequencies of the two red-hair genes in these local populations, not the frequencies of redheads. However, a high figure for the former is likely to lead to increased numbers of the latter in a region unless their red-hair is masked by some other genes involved in hair colour.) And using data from other research studies, the team also got a figure for Ireland of 0.31, the highest uncovered anywhere in the British Isles, and confirmation of that stereotypical image of the red-haired Irishman.

These results are remarkable, as Bodmer acknowledges. 'I was amazed at them. I didn't expect to see something like this.' The point is the research gives us, for the first time, an insight into this aspect of appearance: the startling numbers of native people who have been described as having red hair in ancient times. Famous British redheads include Queen Boudicca, who rebelled against the rule of the Romans and who destroyed and sacked London in AD 60. She was described by the Greek historian Dio Cassius as being 'tall and terrifying . . . a great mass of red hair fell over her shoulders'. Similarly, British slaves were often considered prime purchases – particularly the women – in those days because they often possessed red hair which was highly valued by Romans.

Over the centuries there have been many other famous red-haired Britons, including Elizabeth I, Oliver Cromwell, Nell Gwyn and Winston Churchill. Nevertheless, red locks are mainly associated with only certain parts of the country today, with Scotland being the principal focus in mainland Britain. Prominent 'ginger-heids' – as the Scots describe them – include footballer Gordon Strachan, manager of Celtic; his old friend and rival Alex McLeish, who was manager of Rangers until recently; and the former leader of the Liberal Democrats, Charles Kennedy. Or consider that most potent of all Caledonian icons, the See-You-Jimmy wig. Its prime component is, of course, a mane of ginger hair of ridiculously lavish proportions. The wig is sold as a joke, but there is no doubt that the Scots see themselves as a nation of redheads.

But why do we have such numbers in this part of the British Isles today and not others? Why does it also appear there are also modestly increased numbers of redheads in Cornwall and Devon but not in Sussex or Oxfordshire, as is suggested by Bodmer's work? And why are there all these ginger genes in Orkney but none in Cumbria? The answer, says Bodmer – and many other scientists – is that red-hair genes were common among the first Britons and that populations in the archipelago's fringes still carry their bloodline. 'Genes for red hair first appeared in human beings about 40,000 to 50,000 years ago,' says Rees. These genes were then carried into the islands by the original settlers, men and women who 'would have been relatively tall, with little body fat, athletic, fair-skinned and who would have had red hair,' states David Miles, of English Heritage. Redheads therefore represent the land's most ancient lineages. So if you want an image of how those first people appeared, don't think of a hairy savage with a mane of thick black hair. Contemplate instead a picture of a slim, ginger-haired individual: Prince Harry perhaps, or actress Nicole Kidman (who was born to parents of Scottish and Irish descent).

As for their isolation in Britain's western and northern edges, as well as Ireland, that has much to do with the subsequent history of the British Isles, which we shall discuss in greater depth later in this chapter. For the moment, we should merely note these people ended up in concentrated

*Previous pages:
A selection of British
redheads. Left-hand
page, clockwise from
top left: Boudicca,
Prince Harry,
Elizabeth I,
Catherine Tate
Right-hand page:
Oliver Cromwell,
Patsy Palmer, Nell
Gwyn, Greg
Rutherford*

numbers in the remotest areas of the British Isles, including Cornwall, Devon, Scotland and Ireland, taking their genes with them. The genetic make-up of people in these regions is therefore likely to be the closest to the original founding fathers and mothers. Scientists had suspected so for a long time. Now Bodmer and his colleagues had found compelling evidence to support this idea. For a first set of results, the project scientists could not have done much better.

However, before we leave the subject of red hair it is worth asking why those first Britons had so many men and women in their midst with ginger locks in the first place? Was it an accident? Or is there an evolutionary advantage to having red hair in this part of the world? Intriguingly, the answer to this last question may be 'yes', according to Rees. 'Those MC1R gene variants that incline people to red hair have other impacts on our bodies,' he says. 'In particular, individuals with red hair are, on average, more likely to burn in the sun and are at an increased risk of getting skin cancer.'

The redheads' problem is that they do not make enough of the dark pigment melanin in their skin to protect them against the sun's powerful ultraviolet rays because those MC1R variants have another effect on the skin, as well as their action on hair follicles. 'Essentially, individuals who possess red-hair genes make much less melanin in their skin, and that has important consequences because the pigment provides protection against ultraviolet radiation,' says Rees. 'Thus red-heads are much more prone to blistering. Their skin rarely tans. It just burns or freckles.'

In Africa, where modern humans first evolved 150,000 years ago, such mutations would have been fatal in the searing solar radiation that batters the continent. Dark skin is needed to protect against the powerful ultraviolet radiation of the equatorial sun and to ward off skin cancer. But in northern Europe, the two MC1R mutations would not have posed such a risk given the relatively mild sunshine experienced there.

Indeed, it is even possible that melanin-free skin could have provided its possessors with an advantage in Europe, says Rees, because we make vitamin D in our skin when sunlight shines on it (other sources come from our diet, particularly from seafood). Thus, if you have dark skin and live in a relatively gloomy, cloudy area, your ability to make vitamin D would be badly affected and you could start to suffer vitamin D deficiency. Such individuals tend to develop rickets, in which their bones lose strength and they develop curved legs. Light-skinned people do not have that problem. 'Rickets is not life-threatening today, but it is debilitating,' says Rees. 'Certainly, for a hunter-gatherer, it would have been bad news.' This would have been particularly true for women in whom rickets would have induced pelvic deformations and raised their risk of dying during childbirth. Thus we evolved white, melanin-free skin which has no dark pigment to block sunlight and so will not prevent the production of vitamin D in our skin. Red hair was a side effect.

On the other hand, those MC1R variants may have appeared among our genes by chance and because they caused no real harm in humans, at least while they were living in Europe – so they persisted in the population. 'It is also possible that nature may be fairly indifferent to hair colour in areas of the Earth with low levels of sunshine,' says Rees. 'In that case it is just a matter of diversity triumphing over the odds.'

So there it is: being a redhead could mean you possess an evolutionary advantage over non red-haired people or it could simply be a matter of luck. It is a finely balanced issue, though there has been one recent – and unexpected – development in this story. Work by scientists in the United States and in Britain has uncovered a surprising aspect to having ginger locks. Your susceptibility to pain is reduced compared with others – but only if you are a woman. Researchers have found that red-headed women are better able to tolerate pain than anyone else, including red-headed males. In other words, while blondes may have all the fun, it is the redhead who avoids the pain.

This curious discovery was made in 2003 by geneticist Jeffrey Mogil of McGill University who found painkillers used in childbirth work three times better on red-haired women than on others, or to put it more precisely, red-haired women need doses that are a third of those required for women who have not got red hair. However it is not that pain has anything to do with hair colour, Mogil says. 'It's just that this gene produces a protein and this protein is in the skin where it does one thing and in the brain, where it does something else. The neural circuits that are responsible for pain inhibition are different in males and females. The female pathway simply contains a melanocortin-1 receptor somewhere in it and the male circuit does not.'

Such complexities suggest it is unlikely this phenomenon had much to do with the evolution of red hair in this country. On the other hand, the trait could be important. At the Human Genetics Unit, at the Western General Hospital in Edinburgh, Professor Ian Jackson has launched a study of redheads in the hope of developing new painkillers in the wake of Mogil's discovery. 'Obviously, this finding gives us a new handle on the issue of pain and its control,' he says. 'Our research has already found that the redhead gene particularly affects the way humans experience painful heat and cold. It seems redheads are more sensitive to cold but better able to tolerate intense heat.' On face value, that does not support ideas about evolutionary advantages. Red-headed Scots have to put up with some of the coldest weather in Britain but seem to be the worst equipped for dealing with it. However, it could be argued that this sensitivity to cold could provide an advantage. Those who lack it might allow themselves to get dangerously chilled at times, while those blessed with this temperature sensitivity will be the ones to take avoiding action first, and to survive longer.

However, the discovery has an interesting corollary, adds Jackson:

The sensor that detects heat in our bodies also detects the chemical responsible for the hot taste of chilli peppers. So redheads should be able to tolerate hot spicy food, such as curries, better than other people, and that is what my colleagues and I are preparing to investigate. Our aim is to test concentrations of chillies on people and look for variations in their responses. The expectation would be that redheads can take the highest and hottest concentrations.

Thus our ancient, divergent origins seem to have equipped some Britons with the ability to deal with one of the most powerful challenges of modern life: the vindaloo.

It is unlikely evolution had much to do with this phenomenon, of course. The arrival of Indian cuisine in the British Isles is a relatively recent affair. On the other hand, there is one, rather obscure connection. Geneticists – including Rees – believe Glasgow is probably the repository of the highest frequency of red-hair MC1R variants in mainland Britain, a result of high levels of immigration to the city from Ireland and from western Scotland, and is likely to become a focus for future frequency surveys of MC1R variants. At the same time, the city is known for its Indian cuisine and for its residents' love of a good curry after the pubs close. Could there be a connection? 'It's a very nice idea but I very much doubt it,' says Jackson. 'It's only women who are good at putting up with painful heat and Glaswegian men like a curry as much as its women.'

Nevertheless, being a redhead clearly has its interesting aspects, though we should take a little care about what we mean by the term. There is a whole range of red-headed individuals in this country, including those with auburn hair, strawberry blondes, and simple carrot-tops. These different types of red hair exist because people inherit other hair genes, in particular those that predispose them to have blond or dark hair. These can overpower a person's redheadness and make it hard to spot, for example. This may explain why redheadness is not usually associated with Devon and Cornwall, although it now appears people there do have reasonably high numbers of ginger genes in their midst. Other influences may be helping to camouflage those genes in south-west England. Unfortunately the genetics of these other aspects of hair colouring are poorly understood, thus maintaining a certain amount of confusion over the topic.

The key point about this research, however, is that for the first time it gives a scientific basis to the distribution of attributes that affect people and shows that they do indeed vary round the country. The project has also demonstrated the fate of these early immigrants and has shown that their descendants live on in the nation's corners and edges. The reason why these individuals are concentrated there and are not spread across the nation, is not quite so clear, however. Were they pushed there by waves of newcomers, arriving from the south and east in subsequent millennia? Or was it just that these people didn't mix with these new kids on the block? We shall answer these questions later on but first we need to explore the thorny issue about naming them, the men and women of Scotland, Ireland, Wales and Cornwall. Today, people from these areas are commonly called Celts and when we speak of these perimeter lands, we often call them 'the Celtic fringe'. And certainly their languages – Scottish Gaelic, Irish Gaelic, Welsh, and Cornish – are very similar to each other. (The speaking of Cornish died out in the late eighteenth century although the language was revived in the twentieth and is now spoken by about 3,500 people at a conversational level, and by about 500 fluently. Cornish shares about 75 per cent of its basic vocabulary with Welsh and around 35 per cent with either Irish or Scottish Gaelic.) Gaelic speakers from Scotland and Gaelic speakers from Ireland can understand each other, for example. Similarly, those who speak Cornish can understand the Welsh language. And all four languages share some structure and vocabulary (as they do with a fifth Gaelic language, Breton, which is spoken by people in Brittany). So if we see the greatest concentrations of ancient genes in these places, and also the largest proportion of speakers of Celtic languages, can we conclude that Celtic culture came with the first Britons and that these Gaelic languages are based on the one spoken by the very earliest men and women to inhabit our shores?

The answer to this last question is a simple no. Celtic languages arrived thousands of years after the country was first populated. Nor is it clear that any tribe called Celts or the Celtic lived in the British Isles in the distant past. Indeed the very existence of the Celts – a race who were originally supposed to have come from a great central European empire, and arrived in the British Isles around 600 BC – is now dismissed by most archaeologists and historians. 'Celts have been romanticised into mystical and musical denizens of a never-never land, a sort of Celtic European Union that is supposed to have thrived in prehistoric western Europe,' says David Miles. 'There is absolutely no evidence to support this idea.'

The word 'celtic' comes from the Greek *keltoi* and was first used around the sixth century to describe some of the tribes who lived inland from the Mediterranean and whose ways were considered rough and inferior to those of Athens and, later, Rome. The term applied only to these people. So when Julius Caesar landed in Britain in 55 and 54 BC during his two military missions to the isles, there is no record of him or his generals using the word Celt to describe the natives they encountered. Nor did these people call themselves Celts. In fact, the term did not become popular in Britain until the eighteenth and nineteenth centuries when it was taken up by romantic writers to describe a lost people who lived in these ancient lands and who had been in tune with the true primal forces of nature. William Stukeley, who helped mythologise the Druids and to associate them, wrongly, with the building and use of

Gaelic speaking cultures

☐ Scotish
■ Irish
■ Welsh
☐ Cornish
■ Breton

NORWAY

SCOTLAND

North

Sea

NORTHERN
IRELAND

Irish

IRELAND   Sea

NETHERLANDS

WALES   ENGLAND

BELGIUM

ATLANTIC

English Channel

OCEAN

N

FRANCE

Stonehenge, was the first to describe Britain's ancient monuments as Celtic. Since then, the word has acquired a host of extra meanings, including a particular style of art, a New Age spiritualism, a set of languages, the idea of an ancient, idealistic land of Arthurian gallantry and artistic freedom, and an early form of Christianity. As J.R.R. Tolkein put it: 'Celtic of any sort is a magic bag, into which anything may be put, and out of which almost anything may come.'

The ideal of an idealised Celtic heartland has even been used by nationalist politicians in Scotland, Wales and Ireland to describe a land that was once free of English control (and could be again, it is implied). The term Celtic has therefore acquired a great deal of political and personal baggage. Take this description from Tom O'Neill, a senior writer for *National Geographic*, in an article – headlined *Celt Appeal* – in March 2006.

After listening to a couple of men chatting in a pub on the Isle of Lewis, O'Neill tells us:

> The Sunday mates in the Cross Inn are speaking Scottish Gaelic.
> To them it's not a big deal: it's the first language they learned at home.
> But to me, an American long intoxicated by Irish roots and curious
> whether an even wider and deeper kinship might exist, that of a
> Celtic identity, I felt as if I had stumbled upon a secret society. There
> was something thrilling, even subversive, about hearing an ancient
> Celtic language in the land of Shakespeare, where neither the Queen
> nor the Prime Minister would have the foggiest clue what these locals
> on Lewis were talking about.

These words probably say more about Americans and their attitude to the British than they do about the Irish or Scots, of course. Nevertheless, they convey a flavour of the romanticised, rather confused view many people have about Celts: 'Europe's beautiful losers,' as one writer described this apparently noble but doomed people.

In fact, to many historians, the Celts simply never existed. They point to the Welsh academic and patriot Edward Lhuyd and blame him for triggering the whole Celtic fantasy. In the early years of the eighteenth century, Lhuyd enthusiastically promoted the idea that a great warrior race, the Celtae or Keltoi, had held sway over Europe and had been the scourge of the Greeks and Romans. The Welsh were their direct descendants, Lhuyd added. As the Welsh historian Prys Morgan points out today, this was the first time in 200 years that the Welsh had been presented with a vision of their own history, a version that was autonomous and separate from England's. The idea triggered 'a fashion for the Celts which amount at times to a mania,' as Morgan puts it. Nor was this enthusiasm confined to Wales. It was taken up with equal energy in Scotland and Ireland and other areas of the British Isles, and in some senses, it has never abated. Unfortunately, this vision is largely nonsense. 'The Celts in fact had never by name been associated with the British Isles, but that did not really matter, for they were a magnificent race of conquerors who had thundered across Europe in their chariots,' adds Morgan. 'The Celts reflected the fantasies of the age, and in Wales they provided the constricted, pathetically small nation, which had little to commend it in its present state, with an unimaginably grandiose past, by way of consolation.' Thus it seems the whole notion of a Celtic fringe and an ancient race of British Celts is built on very shaky foundations.

However, we cannot dismiss the use of Celtic terms out of hand, for the simple reason that they have a meaning for many British people today. As I write this chapter, the *Guardian* has just published an article – on the large numbers of Scots, Irish and Welsh viewers who were preparing to watch England's ultimately futile bid to reach the World Cup semi-finals – with the headline: *BBC Edges into World Cup Lead as Celts Tune In*. Clearly, the terms Celts and Celtic have a meaning, one that relates specifically to the people who now live in Ireland and in the western edges of Britain. We cannot then duck the issue and say they did not – and still do not – exist. We can see they are considered to be a viable component of our population by many people. It is also an important issue for our book because the people called Celts are the very ones who carry all those ancient gene variants uncovered in the People of the British Isles project. Some use of the C-word is therefore unavoidable. So if we use it, how should it be applied?

The short-term answer is that we can safely use the word Celtic to describe Gaelic languages and their speakers but no more than that, says Miles. This point is reinforced by Lord Colin Renfrew, the Cambridge linguistics expert. 'The term Celtic should be used to define languages such as Welsh or Gaelic,' he says. 'These languages belong to a class known as the Indo-European Celtic subgroup. Essentially, an early forerunner, or prototype, of these languages was spoken by the first farmers who emerged from the Middle East as they spread across Europe. Eventually, they brought farming, and this language, to the edge of north western Europe.'

Farming slowly filtered across the English Channel as did this proto-Celtic language. Then, as agriculture was gradually taken up in the British Isles, so was this first Celtic language. It then evolved, as it spread, into different versions including the forerunners of Cornish, Welsh, Irish Gaelic and Scottish Gaelic. Slowly the old mother tongue of the ancient Britons was replaced by these Celtic languages which then became the main speech of the British people and would have been used widely when the Romans began their occupation. The first Britons were therefore not replaced by waves of people speaking Celtic languages. Our earliest ancestors simply adopted this new tongue. These languages would have been known as Gaulish, after the Gauls who inhabited mainland Europe in Roman times. To stress our point once more, however, the term Celtic would not have been used at this time.

In later centuries, waves of immigrants – mainly Anglo-Saxon people who spoke a Germanic language – landed in Britain, and took over much of England. Their language evolved into modern English and its speakers expanded in influence across the country. But in the corners of Britain, languages descended from ancient Gaulish – the tongue of the first farming people – lived on. Today, in Scotland, 92,000 people, 2 per cent of the population, speak Gaelic; in Wales 582,000 individuals, 21 per cent, speak Welsh; in Ireland, 1,640,000, about 41 per cent, speak Irish Gaelic. Nearly all these people also speak English, however – most as their first language. (It is also estimated that about 365,000 people speak Breton, 240,000 of them fluently.) 'I don't think it was a matter of these Celtic-speaking Britons being squeezed into the nation's corners,' adds David Miles. 'I think it was simply that they chose not to be Anglo-Saxonised. They just went on doing what they were doing before Anglo-Saxon rule was imposed.' And one of the main things they were doing, of course, was talking in Welsh, Cornish, and Scottish and Irish Gaelic. Thus when we hear these people speak in their rather rhythmic, flowing, slightly guttural speech, we are listening to a language that has been spoken for far longer in the British Isles than English. And many of those words live on over the whole of the British Isles, not just in its Celtic corners. Indeed, they define our landscape and are responsible for many of the basic terms used in this book, as Miles points out. For a start, 'Albion' is a Celtic word. 'Thus early classical navigators came to an island called Albion where the people were known as Pretani,' says Miles. 'This Celtic word probably means the "Painted People" or the "Tattooed Ones". So the first name we have for the people of Britain refers to their fondness for bodily decoration.' (Pretani was later spelled with a B by classical scholars so that the word became Bretani and from that came Britons: painted people.) Similarly names like 'dun', which means fort, is used sixteen times in England and Scotland to name a key place, such as

*A Celtic cross
displaying a typical
design*

Dunfermline, while 'avon', the ancient Gaulish or Celtic word for a river, is used as the name for seven different rivers in Britain.

Thus Celtic tongues have provided us with much of the language we use to describe each other, so we should certainly feel free to use the term, as long as we try not to imbue it with all sorts of ersatz notions of a great lost civilisation or of a Celtic twilight 'that is not so much a twilight of the Gods as a twilight of reason', to quote Tolkein again. In addition, the notion that the nation's western fringes are bonded by a common Celtic culture should be treated with caution, a point stressed by Ken Sweet, the Cornish blood donor for the People of the British Isles project that we

Celtic Pride

Non Harries, another project blood donor, lives in Pembrokeshire, in the village of Dinas Cross, near Fishguard, with her partner and two daughters. 'I wanted to take part in this study because it is incredibly important for me to find out my Welsh roots. My "Welshness" defines me. More than anything else in the world, I am Welsh. My parents were Welsh and their parents were Welsh. I can trace my ancestry in this part of Wales to around 1750 and while I am looking forward to finding some unexpected results about my past, the one thing that is vital is that I find out I have pure Welsh blood.' In short, she is a diehard.

The Harries family is descended from a long line of seafarers. Many of them were captains of merchant ships which they sailed around the world before retiring, with their savings, to Dinas Cross. 'The traditional sum was £2,000. Once you had saved that, you had enough to build a house. The rest you invested – usually in shipping shares – to give yourself an income.' Non lives with her family in a house built by her great-grandfather. But like Ken Sweet, she is finding that life in her area is changing with unsettling speed. 'Most of the houses around here are either second homes for people in cities or they have been bought for outsiders to retire in. In other words, they have come to die here. Ours is one of the last Welsh-speaking households in the village.' But it is Non's views of the rest of the Celtic fringe of Britain that is of particular interest:

> I certainly feel more affinity with these areas – with Cornwall and Ireland and Scotland. I think that has to do with the amount of time our people have all been living in these lands. And that is where the language link comes in. We have been speaking languages like Welsh or Gaelic for much longer than the rest of the country has been speaking English and that binds us in a special way.

met earlier. The credentials connecting him to his native Cornwall are unimpeachable, but he sees no link with himself or his people with those of the rest of the Celtic brotherhood or sisterhood. 'I am Cornish,' he says. 'The Celts are somebody else.'

So, yes, there is a great deal of nonsense talked about Celtic culture and of lost Arthurian kingdoms. But equally it is clear that these people share two quite startling features: they have the oldest bloodline in the country and they speak the oldest languages in the British Isles. That makes them a little bit separate and a little bit special, one would have to concede. Calling them the Celts therefore seems fine as long as you do not assume such individuals come from a long line of Druids.

Thus the concept of the Celts raises important issues about British identity. They give us, whether we like it or not, a convenient name for the very first Britons, men and women who – thanks to the People of the British Isles project – we are now understanding not as dry academic entities but as living individuals with hair, often red, and genes that they have passed on to modern people. Identifying these first settlers to our shores and describing their make-up begs questions, however. Where did these very first Britons come from in the first place? And how did they end up in the British Isles? Did they come from the east, west, north or south? These are critically important issues and we need to take stock of them before we go on to discuss the legacies of more recent immigrants. So let us look now at the story of the first settlers, a tale that takes us deep into the past, to a time tens of thousands of years ago, when the British Isles were an empty, arctic wasteland. For decades, scientists have assumed this era was of little significance. But recently these views have been transformed thanks to remarkable work by geneticists and archaeologists who have shown that this period, which followed the last Ice Age, was probably the most important of all the episodes in our story. Yet despite the passing of millennia, scientists have still managed to link the lives men and women in those days to individuals in the modern world. It is one of the most dramatic parts of our history and is the focus of our next chapter.

CHAPTER THREE

Home Alone

The human brain evidently evolved to commit itself emotionally only to a small piece of geography, a limited band of kinsmen, and two or three generations into the future. To look neither far ahead nor far afield is elemental.

EDWARD O. WILSON, *THE FUTURE OF LIFE*

On Friday 13 November 1993, Roger Pedersen was carefully scraping soil from a trench at an excavation at Boxgrove, in West Sussex. The dig was in its closing stages. Indeed, Pedersen's work was scheduled to be the very last investigation to be carried out at this old gravel quarry, near Chichester. Over the previous ten years, he and dozens of other volunteers had variously sweltered, shivered, and been soaked as they laboured under the guidance of the site's director Mark Roberts, an archaeologist from University College, London. In the process, some of the oldest human artefacts ever found in the British Isles were uncovered at Boxgrove, including hundreds of flint hand axes as well as the bones of carefully butchered rhinos, horses and deer that had been brought down by Stone Age hunters.

It was an impressive hoard. Yet in all that time, Roberts and his colleagues had failed to discover a single anatomical fragment from any of the primitive people who had dominated this patch of land, not even the tiniest scrap of skull or the flimsiest piece of femur. It was this dearth of human fossils that had led to the decision to halt work at the quarry after a decade of excavations. The failure rankled with the Boxgrove team, however, and threatened to sour their forthcoming end-of-dig celebrations.

How Boxgrove Man might have appeared: illustration by John Sibbick

In his trench, Pedersen began pushing back the chalky soil with his trowel. The weather was cold and wet and Pedersen – a retired assembly line worker – was in pain from his arthritis. He was wearing a thick coat, an army sweater, a woollen hat and warm socks but was still shivering in the rain. Nevertheless he worked on and shortly after lunch uncovered a large bone lodged in the chalky sediment. Bones were not uncommon finds at the quarry, of course. Creatures ranging from beavers to bison had left bits of their skeletons there and every piece was considered an important clue to understanding life during Boxgrove's remote past. So Pedersen put the bone – still covered in a block of dirt – in a cardboard box and carried it to the old flint barn that acted as the excavation's headquarters. And there he left it.

For the next couple of days, the box lay undisturbed until Simon Parfitt, the dig's assistant director, took a look inside. He began picking at its coating of soil with the modelling tools he used to probe fossils. Fragments started to flake from the main bone so Parfitt glued them together and after three hours' intense work had reassembled the entire bone minus its coating of soil. He sat back. When Parfitt had started working on the bone, he had expected he would end up looking at the bone of a bear or another of the large animals that had roamed round Boxgrove. But this bone did not come from an animal. Parfitt was staring at a piece of a human being, and a very large, muscular one at that.

Parfitt passed the news on to the rest of the team. 'I was over the moon,' recalls Roberts. To make sure his identification was correct, Parfitt took the find to palaeontologist Professor Chris Stringer, head of the human origins group at the Natural History Museum in London. He confirmed the Boxgrove bone was a piece of human skeleton. 'It was an exhilarating moment,' Stringer recalls. 'It is not very often you come across such an important fossil, particularly one found virtually on your own doorstep.'

What Pedersen had discovered was a tibia, or shin bone, whose ends had been gnawed by a wolf or hyena and which had once belonged to a 500,000-year-old early human of a species known as *Homo heidelbergensis*, a predecessor of modern men and women. To this day, it is the oldest physical remains of a human being that has ever been found in the British Isles. In honour of Pedersen, it was christened Roger,

though its unique status – as Britain's oldest person – did not last long. Saved from closure thanks to that shin-bone discovery, Boxgrove continued to produce more tools and animal bones over the next few years, as well as one other set of items from a human being: two teeth, from a different member of *Homo heidelbergensis*. And that, in the end, is what we possess of the oldest-known inhabitants of the British Isles: a shin bone and a couple of teeth.

The excavation site at Boxgrove

These are meagre rations, to say the least. Yet scientists have still managed to deduce a great deal about their owners, not just from the bone and teeth, but from the tools these people used and from the way they hunted, cut up animals and dominated the landscape. As a result, most experts now rate Boxgrove as the most important ancient site that has been found in the British Isles. From studies, led by Roberts, it is now clear that half a million years ago, the climate was warm and forgiving in this part of the world. Grassland and shrubs covered the region. A land link connected Britain to the continent and Boxgrove was then a raised beach below a 200-foot cliff. A spring fed a freshwater pool at its base. Rhinos, horses, deer and bison came to drink. And lions, hyenas – and humans – came to hunt them.

Boxgrove was a killing floor, in other words, a point demonstrated by one of the most spectacular finds ever made in the old quarry: a horse skeleton with a shoulder injury, a wound that Roberts believes was probably made by a spear. From the plethora of stone chippings found around the quarry, it also seems likely that after the animal was struck, it would have been pounced on and stripped of its flesh within a couple of hours by men and women wielding those hand axes we mentioned earlier. These weapons were thin, heart-shaped, could be held in one hand and were viciously sharp. The term hand axe is a misnomer, however. 'They were never used for chopping down trees,' says archaeologist Francis Pryor. 'So they weren't axes as we know them. The closest modern equivalent would be the light steel cleaver that is used with such skill by

The killing floor at Boxgrove

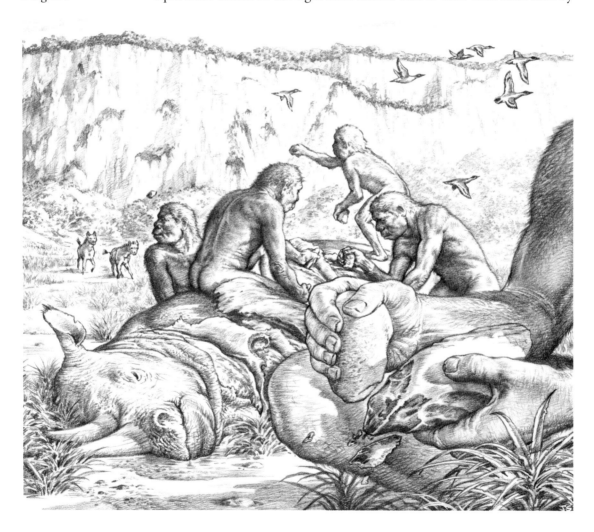

the chefs in Chinese kitchens.' Hand axes were also ten a penny in those day to judge from the hundreds found at Boxgrove. It seems they were chipped from larger stones almost to order, employed briefly – for example to strip away the flesh from that wounded horse – and then discarded. Britain's disposable culture has deep roots, it would seem.

As to the flesh of that horse, some would have been eaten raw on the spot while the horse's bones would have been cracked open with stone hammers to extract its marrow. There would have been competition from other predators, however, including wolves, hyenas and lions. In addition, these butchery sites would probably have become smelly and fly-ridden very quickly. So fillets, chops and bits of offal from the horse may well have been carried to safer ground. 'We don't know if the people of Boxgrove used fire or not,' adds Stringer. 'However, we have evidence from other sites in Britain that fire was being used at least 400,000 years ago, so it is not too fanciful to envisage some of these horse steaks ending up on open hearths.'

The barbecues of Boxgrove: it's a fine image, though we should not get carried away with it. These were no Stone Age suburban garden parties. Filthy and smoky, the fires would probably have been built on safer, higher ground and would have been tended by men and women who would have looked dramatically different from human beings today. That tibia makes it clear that *Homo heidelbergensis* males were muscular, brawny and stocky. They were sprinters not marathon runners. (Scientists estimate that Roger, our Boxgrove Man, was about 5 feet 9 inches tall.) On the other hand, their existences were not 'nasty, brutish and short', as the lives of Stone Age people are commonly supposed to have been. From studies of the tibia's osteones – its bone cells – scientists have calculated its owner was between forty-two and fifty-two when he died, a respectable age for a human given that in those times there was a distinct lack of sanitation or antibiotics or guns to shoot predatory lions. As for the brains of these first people, they were of a fairly imposing size according to fossil skulls of *Homo heidelbergensis* that have been dug up elsewhere in Europe. (The name derives from the first such fossil ever found: a complete lower jaw excavated in 1907 from a gravel pit at Mauer, near Heidelberg, in Germany.) These have cranial capacities of between 1,100 and 1,400cc compared with the 1,300 to 1,600 of modern humans.

Not too much of difference, though not quite the full intellectual monty either. Similarly, the skilful way that Boxgrove folk hunted and butchered animals suggests some cunning and a capacity for careful planning. This point is stressed by the archaeologist the late John Wymer, in a prefix to English Heritage's official report on the Boxgrove site: 'The people were hunters of large mammals; they did hunt with spears; they did retain useful objects for future use … We know that they had craftsmen among them with a concept of symmetry, if not beauty. They performed tasks that involved a division of labour and there is much to imply a social order of groups larger than usually imagined working together.' They were a fairly impressive lot, judged from this perspective. On the other hand, the tools that the people of Boxgrove employed were of a design that had hardly changed for more than a million years. Innovative thinking, the hallmark of *Homo sapiens*, was still beyond them. Roberts remains fairly impressed at their intellectual potential, nevertheless. 'I think if you had stared at Boxgrove Man, it would have been like looking into the eyes of a drunk Glaswegian at midnight,' he says. 'There was definitely something going on, but you couldn't be sure what it was.'

However, it is the appearance of these people that really concerns us. That portrait of Henry VII, discussed in our opening chapter, is the oldest image of a specific, named Briton, created in that person's lifetime, on display in Britain's principal collection of portraits. Since then, artists and computer graphic experts have made many attempts to recreate the looks of people from previous generations, and, in some cases, of individuals from earlier millennia. In the case of Boxgrove Man, however, half a million years separates artist and model, a considerable gulf by any standards. That, of course, makes the end result all the more intriguing, for the reconstruction of this individual has one overriding claim to fame: it is the image of the most ancient Briton of them all. And a very striking and intimidating person he was as well. A single, long bony ridge loomed over his eyes; the forehead sloped back, and the features of the face, in particular, the nose and mouth, were thick and broad. His jaw was massive and so were his cheekbones. His hairline descended well down his forehead, almost to his heavy, bushy eyebrows. Had you met him down some dimly-lit alley, you would have retreated with maximum speed. This would not have been a man with whom one would have trifled.

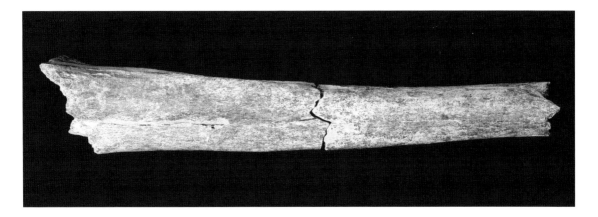

'Essentially, he would have looked like a navvy, and a particularly brutal looking one at that,' says John Sibbick, the British artist who worked closely with the Boxgrove team to create drawings and paintings of the quarry's most famous resident for *National Geographic* and other journals.

The tibia bone of Boxgrove Man which dates back 500,000 years

Some of Boxgrove Man's other features are more difficult to ascertain, however. Human beings had probably lost their body hair by now (or to be more precise, those hairs had thinned) but we have no idea about the colour of the skin that was now exposed. In general, dark skin is thought to be an adaptation to strong sunlight, pale skin to a lack of it, as we noted in the previous chapter. If the people of Boxgrove were longstanding residents, and not recent immigrants from more southerly regions, they may therefore have been relatively light-skinned. As to their eyes, scientists believe blue eyes are a modern evolutionary feature among humans, and so it is likely that these may well have been green- or brown-eyed, though this notion is pure conjecture.

In any case, we should not make too much of our connections with the people of Boxgrove. This lineage, which fought so hard to survive the rigours of ancient Britain, was destined for oblivion, though not for several hundred thousand years. First, *Homo heidelbergensis* began to change across Europe, evolving into a species of thick-set, rugged, big-brained hunters called *Homo neanderthalensis* – the Neanderthals, named after the Neander valley in Germany where the remains of these now extinct species were first discovered in a quarry in 1856. (Technically, the Neander valley finds were not the first pieces of Neanderthal anatomy to be uncovered. At Engis, in Belgium, and at Forbes' Quarry, in Gibraltar, pieces of Neanderthal skeleton had already been dug up in the early nineteenth century, but at the time they were not recognised as belonging to a species different from *Homo sapiens*.)

These enigmatic members of our lineage have left several examples of their tool-making prowess around Britain and Ireland. Chris Stringer, a world authority on the Neanderthals, puts the figure at around two dozen sites:

> That's only for tools, however. When it comes to bones, we have very few: one in Jersey, one in Wales, one in Swanscombe, outside London, and that is about it. It would seem that from all this evidence, the Neanderthals' presence in the British Isles was episodic. When the weather was warm, they might have been a few thousand of them here. When it got bad, as it certainly did during the Ice Ages that swept Europe, they probably abandoned the place completely.

Neanderthals were only part-time residents, it seems. On the other hand, they did make their mark on the islands in some ways. At a gravel pit at Lynford, in Norfolk, archaeologists found in 2002 skeletons of mammoths, rhinos, bison, horses, deer, reindeer, hyenas, wolves, Arctic foxes, and bears and a collection of forty-four beautifully crafted hand axes, made out of glistening black flint. Their edges were still razor sharp. 'They looked brand new,' says David Miles. 'It was a stunning find.' These axes were all of a highly distinctive design known as the bout-coupé, which is found only in Britain, and in one or two places in northern France. These bout-coupé axes suggest Neanderthals in this region had evolved their own distinctive culture and were capable of considerable sophistication. These tools also appear to be the first identifiably British manufactured objects. In other words, the tag, 'Made in Britain', can be traced to Norfolk 60,000 years ago.

The Neanderthals were also great hunters and were far more massive and muscular than modern humans. They also survived the rigours of three separate Ice Ages through which Britain was occupied during its warm periods – as far as can be discerned from the stone tool remains that have been found for these periods. In the end, however, the Neanderthals passed into extinction about 35,000 years ago, huddled in a few strongholds in southern Europe, the 'doomed caretakers of a continent', as writer James Shreve describes them.

The cause of the Neanderthals' demise is still a matter of intense scientific debate, though most experts pin the blame, at least in part, on the arrival, around 40,000 years ago, of a race of upstart émigrés who had travelled out of Africa and into Europe via the Levant. These people were tall and thin with cylinder-shaped bodies that had evolved in a climate in which they needed to maximise heat loss. They were also armed with a new range of sophisticated stone weapons and the capacity to exchange information through complex speech and language. *Homo sapiens* had made it into Europe.

Scientists are still unsure what special conditions led to the evolution of *Homo sapiens* (the name, coined by the eighteenth-century biologist, Carl Linnaeus, means 'wise man') but whatever the causes, the end result was a remarkably canny survivor. Within 5,000 years of modern humans entering Europe, Neanderthals had become extinct. Whether this happened violently, or because our ancestors simply monopolised scarce resources, has still not been settled. To some anthropologists the battle was akin to the ongoing struggle between grey and red squirrels in Britain. One group, grey squirrels, are proving to be just that little bit more flexible in their behaviour and have been resolutely out-breeding their rivals. About 40,000 years ago, a similar fight for resources occurred between humans and Neanderthals, though this time the tussle would have been over access to reindeer and mammoth steaks, not hazelnuts. We just happened to be that little bit lighter on our feet, it would appear. Other scientists, such as the Oxford archaeologist Paul Pettit, see it differently, however. 'For too long we have regarded the extinction of the Neanderthals as a chance historical accident,' he says. 'Rather, where Neanderthals and modern humans could not co-exist, their disappearance may have been the result of the modern human race's first and most successful deliberate campaign of genocide.'

Either way, the effect was final. By around 35,000 years ago, modern humans – who are given the name of Cro-Magnons for this period of European prehistory – were the masters of the continent. (Cro-Magnon means 'big cliff', a reference to the limestone cliff that rises above the town of Les Eyzies, in the Dordogne, where workmen constructing a railway line in 1868 found a single grave containing four Cro-Magnon adults and

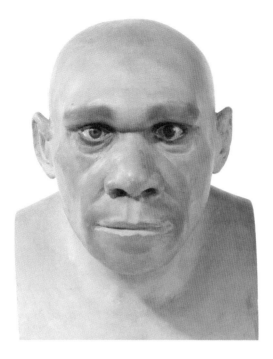
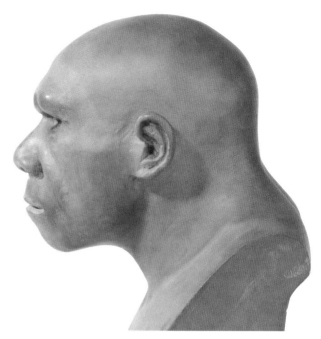

A model head of Homo neanderthalensis

a child.) It did not take the Cro-Magnons long to reach Britain either as can be deduced from a skeleton found at Goat's Hole Cave – at Paviland – on the Gower peninsula in South Wales in 1823 by Rev. William Buckland, Professor of Geology at Oxford, and subsequently Dean of Westminster Abbey. Buckland decreed that the skeleton – which was found under a covering of periwinkle shells, pieces of mammoth ivory as well as 'a coating of ruddle', i.e. red ochre – was that of a 'woman of ill-repute' who had plied her trade among Roman troops based at a nearby camp. As a result the body is still known as the Red Lady of Paviland.

Buckland's interpretation was certainly colourful but it was also completely wrong. In fact, we now know the body is that of the oldest *Homo sapiens* skeleton ever found on British soil. (Only one older piece of modern human anatomy has ever been found in Britain: a fragment of jawbone, found in Kent's Cavern, Devon, which may be up to 35,000 years old.) Radiocarbon dates have shown the Paviland burial is 26,000 years old. Buckland had not stumbled on a Roman prostitute. He had discovered something far more important, as Steven Aldhouse-Green, Professor of Human Origins at the University of Wales, points out. 'When the "Red Lady" skeleton was found, it was the first human fossil recovered anywhere in the world.' Buckland – not surprisingly for

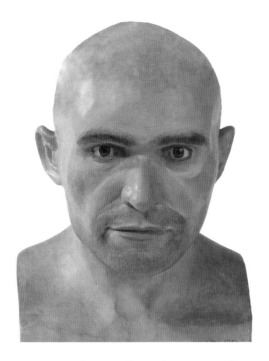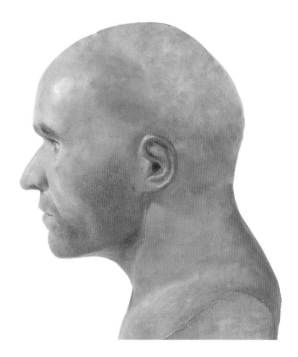

someone working in the early nineteenth century – failed to recognise the skeleton for what it was. More to the point, he also got its sex wrong. The Red Lady was really a man, it transpires.

A model head of Homo sapiens

This reinterpretation of the Red Lady's status is based on a series of studies made during the twentieth century, the most recent having been carried out by Aldhouse-Green. His research has confirmed that the bones closely match the male of our species and not the female. Aldhouse-Green also found that he must have died in his late twenties and was distinctly less robust than his predecessor at Boxgrove. Indeed, his physique was typical of our species: slim – 'gracile' is the term used by palaeontologists – compared either with burly *Homo heidelbergensis* or thick-set *Homo neanderthalensis*. It is estimated that he weighed about 11 stone and was about 5 feet 8 inches tall though this figure is only an approximate one because the skeleton was buried without a skull. Decapitation may seem bizarre but the practice was typical of interments of this period. These are known as Gravettian burials and were carried out across Europe during this time, a period of our prehistory we call the Upper Palaeolithic. It is also possible, says Aldhouse-Green, that the skull might have been washed away when floodwaters swept through Goat Hole Cave at some time after the body had been put in its grave.

Today the Red Lady's grave (the body has been removed to Oxford's Museum of Natural History, much to the disgust of many Welsh nationalists) can only be reached by scrambling down a limestone cliff to an entrance which is accessible at low tide. It was a very different locale 26,000 years ago, however. Then the cave would have been 60 miles from the sea which was far lower than it is today (Britain was again connected by a land bridge to Europe at this time) and would have looked out over plains teeming with prey, including herds of mammoths. And from isotope studies of the Red Lady's bones, it is clear meat formed an important part of his diet, as did plentiful amounts of fish. Indeed, scientists speculate it is possible he and his tribe were in the area to try to catch salmon migrating on the nearby River Severn.

The routes our ancestors took to get into land-locked Britain

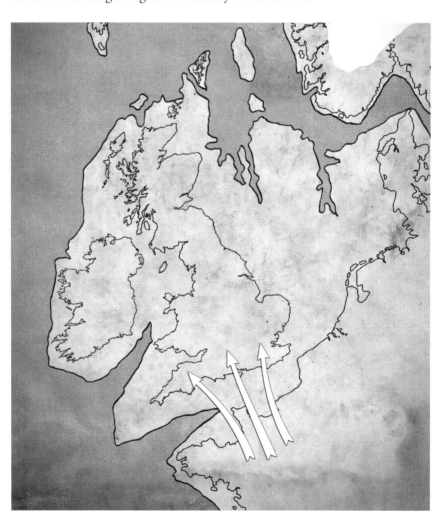

These studies of the Red Lady reveal a picture of a species that was capable of behaving in much more sophisticated ways than those demonstrated by Boxgrove Man. Humans were now displaying considerable adaptability and to judge from the rituals involved in the burial they had also developed a profound interest in religion and the afterlife. Aldhouse-Green argues that the whole area around Goat's Hole Cave was probably sacred and a focus for ancient pilgrimages. His evidence shows the cave was visited regularly by humans for several thousand years beginning about 29,000 years ago. It is likely that priest-like shamans made their attempts to contact the spirit world here, for example, while the Red Lady's grave may have been viewed as some kind of shrine, the Stone Age equivalent of Lourdes or Knock. 'Visits to the cave apparently continued right down to 21,000 years ago in conditions of increased climatic stress,' Aldhouse-Green states in an article, written with Paul Pettitt, that appeared in the journal *Antiquity*. 'These visits, too, are suggestive of the specialness of the site. They also provide a valuable marker for what may have been the last point in time before the human population of the British peninsula was wiped out by climatic downturn or retreated to the refuges of southern Europe.'

Humans had come a long way, in other words. However, as Aldhouse-Green and Pettitt indicate, they were still not destined to settle within the boundaries of the British Isles. Stormclouds were gathering, as can be deduced from a number of factors, not least the lowering of sea levels that was going on at this time. Dropping ocean surfaces could mean only one thing: that much of the world's water was now being locked up in ice sheets growing at the North and South Poles. Remorselessly, these great rivers of frozen water spread to lower and lower latitudes as the world cooled, until, by around 20,000 years ago, the planet was gripped by an Ice Age in full spate. So much water would have been locked up in the northern hemisphere's ice cap that sea levels would have dropped dramatically, turning the bed of the North Sea into a vast expanse of tundra, now known as the North European Plain. Only a narrow channel would have divided Scotland from Scandinavia while the Hebrides, and Orkneys would all have been part of mainland Britain. At the same time, Scotland was covered by glaciers as was much of Ireland, Wales and northern England while temperatures dropped until they reached levels that were 5 degrees Celsius lower than today's. Throughout Britain, human beings made themselves scarce – and for some time. Despite intensive searching, scientists have not been able to find a single sign of human habitation in the British Isles between 21,000 years and 15,000 years ago. The land was either crusted in great sheets of ice or had been turned into tundra that was swept by howling gales and blizzards.

Humanity had not gone far, however. Thanks to a remarkable research project, linking the talents of fossil experts, geneticists and statisticians, researchers have recently tracked these ancient Europeans to their Ice Age lairs and studied how they behaved, first as the world cooled, and later as it warmed up again. This episode in our prehistory turns out to have been a critical one in establishing the make-up of the people of Britain. Indeed, scientists believe it was the single most important event in the establishment of the population of the British Isles. Our ideas that Anglo-Saxon invasions and Viking hordes had major impacts on our make-up are not misguided, it should be stressed. But what occurred 15,000 to 16,000 years ago in this corner of Europe dwarfs even these great historical events. Even more extraordinary has been the discovery – based on careful analyses of numbers of fires, tools, and bones left behind at all the sites in the region – that only a few hundred people were involved, probably men and women belonging to a few extended families. These were the people who headed north, from south-western Europe, as the Ice Age ended and the glaciers retreated, and moved into the empty terrain of Europe's British peninsula. For the rest of this chapter, we shall look at the details of these defining days, which determined what sort of people the inhabitants of the British Isles would become.

The first key questions to be addressed are relatively straightforward ones, however. Just where did those elusive members of *Homo sapiens* go when the climate turned nasty? Where did they choose to spend the long winter that had settled over Europe? The answers are equally simple, but somewhat surprising. Our ancestors selected the very parts of Europe to which Britons still retire when the weather gets unbearable in their home country. They went to Spain and the south of France.

Professor Clive Gamble of Royal Holloway University, London, explains:

Beginning around 25,000 years ago, as climatic conditions across the continent got worse and worse, humans began settling in some numbers along the north coast of Spain, in areas around Santander and San Sebastián today, and along rivers in the Dordogne area of France. We can see the stone tools they left behind in caves and rock shelters and the campfires they made. Then, as the weather got even colder, and ice sheets spread down from the north, they confined their activities to smaller and smaller patches of territory around these refuges. Essentially, they sat out the last Ice Age here. A few young men might have occasionally gone off on a hunting trip for a few weeks to bag the odd mammoth to impress the girls back home. Apart from that there wasn't much going on outside the refuge areas.

Herds of reindeer were important sources of protein for Stone Age Britons

This picture has been built up by a team of researchers led by Gamble, and Professor Martin Richards of Leeds University, and has involved scientists in making comprehensive surveys of all Cro-Magnon sites in Western Europe. From these studies, data about tool use, radiocarbon dates, animal bones, and other factors were collected, carefully plotted on graphs and subject to detailed analysis. 'We can see quite clearly from these studies that for millennia, nothing happened outside the refuge areas in northern Spain and southern France,' says Gamble. 'Then, about 16,000 years ago, there is a sudden burst of activity. Camps start appearing along routes that lead round France's Massif Central – which would still have been inhospitably cold – and head straight towards the great valley in which we now find the English Channel and on to land that has since become the British Isles.'

Gamble and Richards estimate there would have been a maximum of 9,000 men, women and children in these Western European refuges at this time. Most remained where they were in the relatively balmy south with only a few families of pioneers taking part in the great race north, an estimate that is backed by studies of the sizes of the campsites they left en route. This paucity of numbers has crucial implications for our understanding of the population of the British Isles, as we shall see.

It is also worth noting that these people, 'this happy few', were not marching north with the aim of bagging prime pieces of unoccupied real estate before anyone else got to them. All they were doing was extending the ranges of their activities – in particular, their hunts for horse and reindeer. These animals were the prime sources of protein, the Palaeolithic equivalent of the Big Mac. As herds moved north, humans would have followed. It is also worth noting that these peregrinations parallel the early diaspora of humanity out of Africa which we discussed in the first chapter of this book. Around 100,000 years ago, it was a bit like wandering down the beach to get away from the crowd, as we noted. This time it was more like a stroll down an empty valley to find a better spot for a bit of hunting or fishing. It is a point stressed by the anthropologist Jonathan Kingdon. 'The movement or expansion of people over considerable distances is often imagined as if prehistoric groups were seized by the urge to explore or migrate,' he says. 'Such movements did not depend on individual wills; it was external events. A succession of bad years, incursions by aggressive neighbours, overpopulation, over-hunting, the invention of new and superior techniques, fleeing from disease, or fulfilling the prophecies of a shaman; all these and more could have triggered movement on and into the unknown.'

Whatever the reason for its initiation, this particular trek took our ancestors up the valleys of the Rhône and Saône rivers into the land around the western lakes of Switzerland and then up the valley of the Rhine. At all times, of course, these people were moving into totally unpopulated territory, a forbidding landscape that would have been harsh and unwelcoming but which must have carried some hint of Palaeolithic promise. 'These routes acted as Stone Age motorways,' adds Gamble, 'especially when people got going up the Rhine, then they really put their feet down. They moved north at an incredible pace.'

It is an intriguing picture, one of a species, poised – almost straining – to break out of the confines of south-west Europe as soon as the weather permitted. Gamble says:

> It's certainly a neat image. However, there is one problem with it and that concerns the issue of timing. By studying sediment samples taken from the Atlantic seabed, we get very precise estimates of temperatures across Europe over the past few hundred thousand years and these show the continent was still gripped by Ice Age conditions 16,000 years ago – just at the time that humans were breaking out of their refuges. Europe remained very cold for the next 1,000 years. What set off these people is therefore difficult to fathom. Probably they could read cues of impending climatic improvement that we cannot detect today. It is a mystery, however.

Nevertheless, it is clear that by 15,000 years ago mankind had reached the British peninsula of what would become the British Isles once more and had begun to establish camps across its southern reaches. It was not a process of setting up permanent homes and putting down roots, however. It was more likely that every few years these itinerant hunter-gatherers would venture to the extreme northern edge of their ranges, thus taking them on to the peninsula. Then, as the weather got better, they went every two years, then every year. 'Then one day they took granny and the kids and set up a semi-permanent camp in this new territory. That is how Britain would have been populated,' adds Gamble.

There was the odd hiccup, however. Around 12,500 years ago, there was an abrupt reversal in the slow warming of Europe and temperatures again plunged. This sudden cooling is known as the Younger-Dryas event and has been traced to a huge outburst of melted glacier water from central north America. Effectively, this switched off the Gulf Stream that was just beginning to help to heat up Europe. 'A sea ice cap formed within short order, preventing the Gulf Stream from starting up again, helping to trigger an intensely cold climatic regimen in Europe,' says Brian Fagan, an anthropologist based at the University of California, Santa Barbara. 'The cold endured for ten centuries.'

In Britain, this great cooling event is known as the Loch Lomond cold phase, after the Scottish loch whose banks provided the first evidence for its existence. Once more glaciers returned to the Scottish Highlands, covering them in huge tongues of ice; winter sea-ice stretched down the western British peninsula and on to France and Spain; while most of the landscape would have turned to tundra once more. However, the climate did not deteriorate quite so badly as it had during the Ice Age and mankind managed to cling on in Britain. We know this from at least one key find. In 1982, a strangely worked tool made of reindeer antler – which looks for all the world like a modern policeman's baton – was discovered at a quarry at Earls Barton, in Northamptonshire. Batons like these are called Lyngby Axes and had previously been dug up at sites in

Reindeer antlers were used as tools

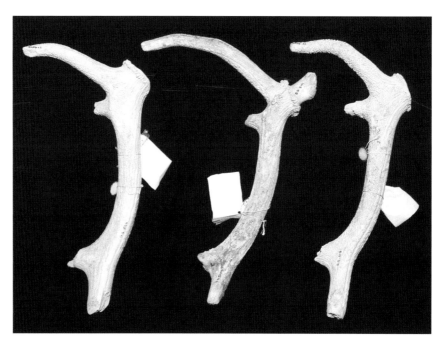

Germany, Poland and Holland. Again the term 'axe' is a misnomer. It's now clear these instruments were never used for cutting. Indeed, it is uncertain what they were used for though they could have been used to work leather or plant materials. The crucial point is that the Earls Barton 'axe' has been dated at being around 11,000 years old. At this time, of course, the Loch Lomond phase probably still held the peninsula in its freezing grip, so humans were managing to survive this harsh landscape, though they may not have been having a lot of fun in the process. Then, a few hundred years later, the climate improved again and populations began to expand again across the country and our hunter-gatherer ancestors took control of the peninsula again.

Gradually more and more areas of the peninsula were explored by nomadic hunters as they followed their herds of reindeer and horses into new lands and eventually the first of these people reached Scotland. It is worth noting, however, that when we refer to these first Brits as hunter-gatherers, it was the former occupation that took precedence over the latter. Most of today's surviving hunter-gatherer tribes live in relatively warm zones and berries, tubers, nuts and other vegetation provide most of their food. An occasional 'kill' of an animal then provides a protein boost to their diet. However, in Britain, plant foods would not have got near to providing the calories these people would have needed for survival. So hunting would have taken on a special significance and meat would have formed the major portion of people's diet. On the other hand, the Brits have always loved a good steak.

Then, around 9,500 years ago, the geological processes that were to have such a profound role in shaping the British Isles and their inhabitants entered a critical phase. At this time, the waters of the Rhine, Seine and Thames poured into one massive river that ran through a great valley westward to the Atlantic Ocean. This estuary divided terrain that would become southern England from the territory that would form northern France. Inexorably the estuary was expanding. 'Sea levels were rising at a rate of about 10 mm a year as the planet warmed and ice caps melted,' says Professor Ian Shennan of Durham University. 'Shorelines would have been continually moving inland and salt marshes would have been forming along the edges of the estuary.' Shennan and his colleagues recently created a computer reconstruction of these events. These show

How the Britain became an island: 10,000 years ago, the land was linked by low-lying plains to Europe; by 8,000 years ago, a channel had formed and separated the British Isles from the continent; 6,000 years ago, the isles were much as they are today; and by 4,000 years the British Isles reached their present state

that by around 9,000 years ago, the English Channel was now a sea passage that separated Britain from France. There still existed a land link with the continent, however – a stretch of low-lying plain that connected northern Norfolk with Holland. 'We can tell from the peat we extract from the seabed that there were oak forests there,' adds Shennan. 'Slowly these would have died out as the salt marshes spread and the water rose.' Eventually by about 8,300 years ago, this connecting strip of land had disappeared beneath the tides and Britain was now an island (though for another 500 years, the area in the North Sea known today as Dogger Bank, would have been an island, known as Doggerland and was probably inhabited). Thus this obscure corner of Europe was transformed from a peninsula into a 'precious stone set in a silver sea', an act that was to define the British character indelibly. From now on, everywhere else was overseas.

In this way, a subset of European hunter-gatherers, who had inhabited the British Isles gradually between 15,000 and 11,000 years ago, and then in some numbers between 10,000 years and 8,500 years ago, suddenly became the sole rulers of a new landscape and possessors of a now isolated gene pool. 'There would have been some continued genetic input from immigrants, particularly from the south-west of Europe where there seems to have been fairly constant maritime interaction,' says Gamble. 'Nevertheless, these people became the founding mothers and fathers of modern Britons.'

Starting from only a few thousand, the islands' population expanded

6,000 years ago   4,000 years ago

– albeit very slowly at first, according to estimates made by the British archaeologist Christopher Smith. During the Loch Lomond phase, there would have been no more than 1,100 to 1,200 people on the peninsula. By around 10,000 years ago, as the weather warmed, things began to pick up and the population may have reached 2,400. By around 9,000 years ago, there would have been between 2,500 and 5,000. These are remarkably low numbers, compared with the 62.9 million people that live here today, a figure based on 2002 estimates of the population of the British Isles. Great Britain, the largest island, has a population of 57.1 million while Ireland, the second largest has 5.7 million inhabitants. The two other main groups of islands are the Channel Islands, with 149,993 inhabitants, and the Isle of Man, which has 76,315.

The major change that occurred, of course, was the appearance of farming around 6,000 years ago, a monumental revolution that we shall discuss in the next chapter. All we need note now, however, is that by the time of the invasion of the Romans, in AD 43, the British Isles probably had up to 3 million inhabitants. Crucially, there has been no real massive input of genes to change that make-up, with one controversial exception which we shall discuss in Chapter Five. The key point is that people of the British Isles are more or less the same as they were 10,000 years ago. Yes, there is some variation concerning red hair and blood groups and Y-chromosomes, differences that are helping us to unravel the details of our prehistoric past. But the basic genetic manuscript on which our past has been recorded is that of ancient hunter-gatherers. We are all Stone Age men and women under the skin, it seems. This point is backed by David Miles, chief archaeological adviser to English Heritage. 'There was a lot of arguing in the 90s and early part of the 21st century about this issue, but it is now more or less agreed that about 80 per cent of Britons' genes today come from hunter-gatherers who came in immediately after the Ice Age,' he says.

The debate to which Miles refers concerns the idea – accepted for much of the latter part of the twentieth century – that there was a considerable input of genes into Europe from the people who brought farming from the Middle East. Eastern European hunter-gatherers would have been the first to come into contact with these farming arrivistes and would have absorbed their genes for longer. In the west, it would have taken longer, and the genetic mixing would have been more dilute. Nevertheless, the theory suggested a significant input of genes from eastern farmers should be found in men and women in the British Isles today. This is known, by some scientists, as the replacement theory and states that farming brought such critical advantages to its practitioners that their numbers expanded explosively and overwhelmed the continent's sparse numbers of hunter-gatherers. We are really farming folk underneath it all, it is argued. Not so much a replacement theory, more the Ambridge vision of the peopling of Britain. Those who possessed Archer genes prospered in their lavish farms while the Grundy clan – hunter-gatherers to a man and woman, one would have thought – became the dispossessed.

However, the idea has not fared well in recent years. Studies, like those of Gamble and Richards, suggest that the input of eastern farmers into the gene pool of the British Isles, and indeed for much of Europe, was negligible. Richards and his colleagues used a complex analysis of hundreds of samples of mitochondrial DNA taken from people from all over the continent to demonstrate this point. Mitochondrial DNA is important because it is inherited only through the maternal line. My mitochondrial DNA is the same as my mother's, and her mother's, and her mother's mother's, and so on back into the mists of humanity's past. A father's mitochondrial DNA is never passed on, however, and always ends up on the cutting-room floor during the processes of reproduction.

Thus my children – Anna, Tom and Olivia – all have the same mitochondrial DNA as my wife, Sarah, who of course got hers from her mother. In turn, Anna and Olivia will pass that mitochondrial DNA on to their children. So think of mitochondrial DNA as being a little bit like Jewishness. Both are inherited from mothers. However, the crucial point is that this unbroken matriarchal lineage can be exploited to reveal the secrets of our biological past. Mitochondrial DNA slowly accumulates mutations at a fairly reliable rate and that makes it possible to establish accurate chronologies for maternal lineages created through use of this type of genetic material. In this way, it becomes possible to reveal the ancestry of different maternal lineages, the relatedness of these lineages, and the times at which these lineages branched to form new ones.

Richards and his team took the samples they had collected and processed them, using computers, to see if they formed clusters. In other words, they tested these DNA samples to see if there were any common versions of particular mitochondrial loops containing the same or similar mutations. There were. The team found a number of clearly identifiable clusters of mitochondrial DNA in the people of modern Europe. Then they looked at the ages of the founding of these groups which they could calculate by counting the small number of mutations that these clusters had acquired. Nearly all the clusters turned out to be older than 10,000 years, dates that long preceded the arrival of agriculture in Europe. In other words, these lineages had flourished when farmers were supposed to have been overwhelming sparse populations of hunter-gathers. There was no sign of the replacement of the hunter-gatherers of the British Isles and Europe by farmers and a great deal of evidence to suggest the former flourished and established lineages that persist through the population of the British Isles today. It was not the farmers who advanced across Europe all those years ago, it seems. It was the idea of farming that travelled. Its impact was profound, of course – but only in cultural, not genetic terms.

But if our past was so heavily influenced by hunter-gatherer opportunists, there should be some direct evidence of their impact in our gene-pool today, an idea that was to be tested with unexpected results in the late 1990s by Professor Bryan Sykes of Oxford University, a member of Richards's team. At the time, Sykes – and many other researchers at different institutions – was learning how to use the awkward techniques involved in testing ancient mitochondrial DNA from skeletons and corpses. Among the different technologies involved in these techniques is PCR – or DNA amplification. It is a very powerful technique, as we have seen, but can cause headaches for researchers. In particular, contamination from scientists' own DNA has proved to be a constant source of difficulty. Nevertheless, once these problems have been overcome, DNA amplification has proved to be an instrument of extraordinary power for studying our prehistory.

Sykes was looking for a case to demonstrate this potential and picked on the Cheddar Man, one of the most striking prehistoric finds ever made in Britain. In 1903, the remains of a young man had been found, with his feet curled up underneath him, in Gough's Cave, a spectacular cavern system in the Cheddar Gorge in Somerset. We now know this to be the oldest, complete skeleton of a member of *Homo sapiens* ever found in the British Isles. Importantly, the skeleton – unlike that of the Red Lady of Paviland – had a skull. In addition, cut marks on his bones are very similar to those left by human hunters when stripping an animal of its flesh. As a result, they have suggested Cheddar Man may have been ritualistically eaten after death, possibly by members of his own family as an act of veneration. 'This wasn't the casual consumption of human flesh as a lazy substitute for, say, a haunch of venison when the larder was empty,' says Francis Pryor. 'No, it was something ceremonial, symbolic and special. It could have been an act of hostility to a vanquished foe, but more likely it was an act of respect to a departed relative.'

The crucial point about the Cheddar Man is that his death – 9,000 years ago according to radiocarbon dating – puts him in line to be one of the hunter-gatherer founders of the people of the British Isles. (By this time, the islands had left the Palaeolithic or Early Stone Age and were now in a period known as the Mesolithic, or Middle Stone Age.) But could Sykes find a connection between him and modern humans? It was a task ideally suited to the technology of DNA amplification. So Sykes went to work. First he tried to extract DNA from the Cheddar Man's bones but failed to get any material. So Sykes, working with Chris Stringer, in whose Natural History Museum vaults the skeleton is stored, hit on the notion of trying to remove mitochondrial DNA from one of the skeleton's teeth. (These teeth were in better condition than Sykes's

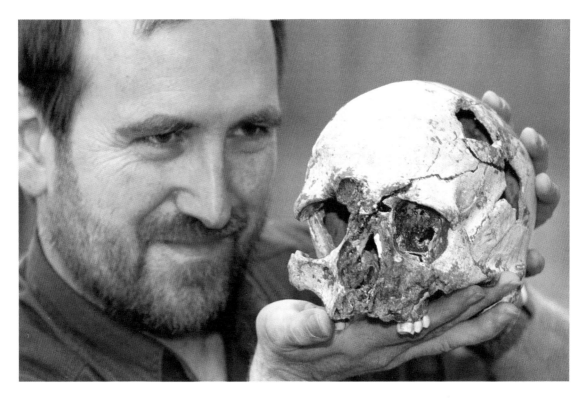

own dentures, the scientist later observed, a reflection – it could be argued – of the healthiness of the hunter-gatherer way of life.) The idea worked. Sykes extracted a total of 200 milligrammes of a cream-coloured powder from the centre of one of the Cheddar Man's molars. This was more than adequate for his needs and proved to be rich in mitochondrial DNA. Sykes grew up copies of key sections of this DNA in his Oxford laboratory and compared it with mitochondrial DNA of people today. It provided a perfect match with one of the mitochondrial clusters that Richards and his team had uncovered in modern Europe. 'The ancient DNA from Gough's Cave was completely modern,' recalls Sykes. 'The sequence is by far the commonest in Europe and here we had found it in the tooth of a young man who had lived thousands of years before the arrival of farming in Britain. The Palaeolithic gene pool had not been fatally diluted by Middle Eastern farmers. There was more of the hunter in us than anyone had thought.' This point is backed by David Miles. 'Rather than tidal waves of invasions scouring the genetic beach of Britain, results like Gough's Cave suggest a basic continuity of population from the Upper Palaeolithic,' he says.

The skull of Cheddar Man being held by Chris Stringer of the Natural History Museum

The DNA discovery was certainly exciting. But Sykes took his project a stage further by taking DNA samples from children and teachers at the Kings of Wessex Community School, near Gough's Cave, and compared its key sections with the mitochondrial DNA he had found in the teeth of Cheddar Man. Sykes got three matches: two pupils and one adult, Adrian Targett, one of the school's history teachers.

It is a truly compelling story, one that connects two individuals that lived in different millennia. And that, of course, is what fascinates about this use of DNA.. It may be interesting to be told that people like the Cheddar Man would have appeared like humans today and, if put in a suit would have been indistinguishable from our office colleagues. But it is utterly compelling to know that a schoolmaster shares the same DNA

Cave Connection

Adrian Targett, whose genes were found to match the mitochondrial DNA of the Cheddar Man, admitted he was astonished when told by scientists that he was a descendant. 'It is very strange news to receive,' he told reporters. The story was printed in every British national newspaper, from *The Times* to the tabloids. *Yaba dada doo!: Genes prove teacher's old man's a caveman*, announced the *Mirror*, while the *Daily Telegraph* went for the simple but effective: *Cheddar Man is my long-lost relative.* Best of all, however, was the *Sun's I'm Barney Double: Teacher Adrian is related to caveman 9,000 years old.*

Targett became a celebrity overnight and was even asked by one of Britain's tabloids to pose – for a five-figure sum – in a loincloth beside the full-size reconstruction of the Cheddar Man that stands in the gorge today. Fortunately, for his continued good standing in his neighbourhood, Targett declined. There was also much media attention given to Targett's admission that he was fond of having his steaks cooked rare, as if the mitochondrial DNA he had inherited somehow imbued him with an atavistic urge to eat raw meat. This was certainly not the case. That mitochondrial signal merely indicates the presence of a loose genetic link with our ancestors, not as a 9,000-year-old caveman and that a little slice of the latter's genes have passed through 300 generations of people who lived in the same neighbourhood. Such revelations give a visceral feel for the antiquity of the British people and of the slender, precious strand that links us with our ancestors.

There are other points to stress, however. For a start, Adrian Targett is an only child, so his immediate family's contribution to this mitochondrial DNA has come to an end. The same was true, of course, of the Cheddar Man. His mitochondrial DNA also terminated with him. However, it is likely he will have had at least one living female relative with whom he shared his mitochondrial inheritance, a woman whose lineage zigzagged through the generations until it reached the mother of Adrian Targett.

a hard-wired instruction to behave as they did. On the other hand, it is easy to appreciate the widespread national fascination with the story of Targett and the Cheddar Man: a local schoolteacher and a Stone Age caveman sharing a neighbourhood – and a common ancestor 9,000 years ago.

A reconstruction of Cheddar Man

Alternatively, the lineage of the Cheddar Man could have died out with him. Then someone else with the same mitochondrial DNA – which scientists have already shown to be common in Europe – came to the area in later centuries or millennia and re-established the lineage that led to Targett.

However, the most important point about the story of Adrian Targett and Cheddar Man goes back to the issue of the arrival and impact of farming, as Larry Barham, an archaeologist, stressed. The discovery of a 9,000-year-old unbroken genetic lineage in Britain again provides strong support for the idea that we are a land of hunter-gatherers and not a nation of farmers. 'The discovery of the link between modern Somerset people and the Cheddar Man adds to the evidence that Britons came from a race of hunter-gatherers who later turned to farming because they found it was to their advantage,' he says. 'In the past, there was an assumption – by some scientists – that hunter-gatherers were somehow intellectually not up to the mark and that they did not have the savvy of the farmers that came later to our shores. But it wasn't like that, we now know. Hunter-gatherers were every bit as sophisticated as the farmers, clever enough to expropriate the agricultural ideas they found useful.'

For his part, Sykes had one more trick up his sleeve. Having achieved such a coup in linking ancient and modern Britons through Cheddar Man's extended family, he attempted to do the same for an even more august predecessor of the British people, the Red Lady of Paviland. This was a tougher nut. At almost three times the age of Cheddar Man, it offered far poorer prospects for providing meaningful stretches of genetic material. Like all materials, DNA decays and the older a human sample, the less chance there is of extracting intact stretches of mitochondrial DNA. Nevertheless, Sykes succeeded in extracting 39 milligrammes of bone powder from the femoral cortex of the Red Lady and managed to isolate a small sequence of mitochondrial DNA. It turned to be the same as the sequence that was found in Cheddar Man. Our hunter-gatherer roots run very deep, it would seem.

However, there is one important caveat that should be noted about these two stories – of the Red Lady and of the Cheddar Man. Although Sykes announced he had found links between both individuals and modern DNA clusters, he has never published his results in a peer-reviewed scientific journal. Many scientists find this frustrating. As several have pointed out, research into ancient DNA is bedevilled with problems of contamination and other issues. In publishing his full results, Sykes would demonstrate how he achieved his matching of the Cheddar Man with the modern world.

In any case, the crucial point about this part of our story is that it makes it clear that for most of the past half a million years – when Britain and Ireland were occupied sporadically by humans of various types – these lands were not islands but were the extreme peninsula of a continent undergoing wide-ranging climatic and biological change. Then, just as one of these great population experiments was in full swing, and Britain was being peopled by one very small subset of *Homo sapiens*, the waters rose up and cut off the land, and its new inhabitants, from the rest of Europe. This isolation was not absolute, of course. Strangers and immigrants continued to arrive in trickles, and on one or two occasions in waves, and so started a process of subtle variation in the pool of red-hair genes and DNA variants that had been established by the first British people. These are the subjects for succeeding chapters. Before we look at these, however, we need to examine the impact of farming when it did eventually reach our shores, around 6,000 years ago.

Agriculture represents a major technological change for the world, not just the British Isles. Indeed, it can be argued it was the invention with the most profound impact in the history of humanity. To some historians, it was the start of a great new era of order and progress. Freed from the continuous toil of finding food, men and women were able to begin to investigate our planet and the universe. To others, it was simply the worst project in the world, an experiment that doomed mankind to the tyranny of ownership, subservience and disease. So let us examine how this extraordinary experiment affected the people of the British Isles and look at its prime practitioners, the people who set in motion changes that were to turn the land into one of the world's richest pieces of agricultural real estate.

CHAPTER FOUR

From Hazelnuts to Henges

Man is the only creature that consumes without producing.
He does not give milk, he does not lay eggs, he is too weak to
pull the plough, he cannot run fast enough to catch rabbits.
Yet he is lord of all the animals.

GEORGE ORWELL

L ondon's £2-billion Channel rail link with Europe was one of the
most expensive and demanding engineering projects carried out
in recent times. Dozens of new bridges and tunnels were
constructed; boring machines, each 120-metres long, and weighing more
than 1,000 tonnes, were employed to drill tunnels; entire new stations
were built at Ebbfleet and Stratford; while London's Victorian St Pancras
station was transformed into a glittering international terminal. The line
can now carry trains at speeds of more than 180 mph on the 67-mile
journey from capital to coast.

These works were a dream for rail enthusiasts. Surprisingly, they were
also good news for archaeologists. In the process of digging the rail link's
banks, tunnels and cuttings, a hoard of prehistoric treasures were
uncovered by teams of workers who were specifically hired to study, and
rescue, finds uncovered during the rail link's excavations. As Martin
Wainwright, writing in the *Guardian*, put it: 'This was the longest,
narrowest and potentially richest archaeology dig in Britain.' The track,

and its tunnels and cuttings, created a 200-foot wide slice through the Kent countryside, and along its length key discoveries were made, on average, every half a mile. It was 'like a long string of pearls', says Helen Glass, archaeology manager for Rail Link Engineering, the company responsible for the line's construction. Riches uncovered this way included a Roman villa, a medieval moated manor house, an ammunition dump from the Second World War, a horde of mummified cats (which had been hidden in a building to deter evil spirits) and a Stone Age flint factory.

However, for archaeologists the most intriguing find of all was made at Blue Bell Hill, near Rochester, in Kent. Here they found a series of holes that had once held posts for a wooden longhouse that was dated, using radiocarbon tests, as being almost 6,000 years old. The building – known as White Horse Stone House – turned out to be massive: 18 metres long and 8 metres wide, and stood high on the North Downs overlooking a plain below. 'The builders created a clearing in the forest so

The construction of the Eurostar rail link from London to the coast revealed a host of important archaeological sites

that they could erect the longhouse, which was then in use for about a century,' says David Miles. However, it was not so much the size of the house, as its shape that aroused the interest of archaeologists. Native houses of this period were circular. White Horse Stone House was rectangular. 'In fact, this style of construction – a longhouse – was common on the continent at the time,' adds Miles. 'There is a good cause to regard this as one of the very first British farm buildings, built in a style used by those who had imported agriculture.'

Such a find is of enormous scientific value. It is also one of considerable symbolic importance, for the introduction of farming was probably the main technological change to affect life in the British Isles in the past 15,000 years, greater even than the massive transformations of the Industrial Revolution. Agriculture turned a sparsely populated group of islands, which probably supported a few thousand individuals, into an intensively cultivated landscape that would – in a relatively short space of time – provide homes for more than a million people. By any standards, that was a revolutionary change. We ceased following herds of animals and instead fenced them into enclosed spaces where we could use them at our leisure. Similarly, we stopped wandering round to find a berry here or a root there and grew plants in fields where we could tend them. Farming brought security to the provision of food and allowed people to pursue other activities, resulting ultimately, in the scientific and technological advances that have produced medicine, space travel and the means to explore our past. However, it also introduced the concept of land ownership and triggered an exponential rise in populations that have taken human numbers in the British Isles to almost 63 million and across the world to almost 6.5 billion. Many of the planet's ecosystems have been destroyed, as a result. Farming has brought as many curses as blessings to the British Isles and to the rest of the world. So let us examine these effects, both good and bad, and look at the way farming arrived on these shores and how it affected the land and its people.

However, before we begin our exploration we need to look at the way our ancestors were living before these momentous events swept the islands. In addition, we need to consider our use of chronological terms. In previous chapters, we spoke of dates in terms of numbers of 'thousands of years ago'. Archaeologists and historians usually switch to BC around

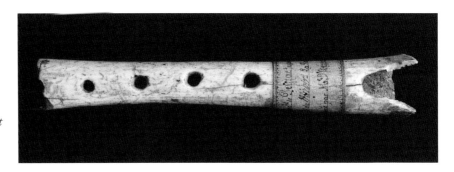

A flute sculpted from bone, one of the oldest musical instruments ever found

this period of history, however. Thus we need to subtract 2,000 from each date we encounter, remove the words 'years ago' and add the initials BC instead. Thus the date of the construction of that house at Blue Bell Hill 6,000 years ago becomes 4,000 BC. As to the nature of life in Britain before the arrival of farming, it would still have been harsh. The life of a hunter-gatherer during a typical British winter could not have been fun. On the other hand, there would have been compensations. Our forebears – to judge from the behaviour of the world's few surviving tribes of hunter-gatherers – would probably have had far more hours of leisure compared with men and women today. Work would have been restricted to hunting and gathering food, while life in clans and tribes – which would have numbered between 50 to 300 people – would have been unstructured and free of the authoritarian strictures of twenty-first century life. 'Such bands and tribes were relatively egalitarian,' says Miles. 'Leaders were occasionally chosen on the basis of experience or charisma to head war bands or delegations. But most work parties were self-selecting, shared their spoils in common and people held little in the way of private property. These people were the original, and genuine, communists.' Indeed, life round ancient fires could have been quite jolly to judge from other finds that have been made on the continent. Humans, it seems, had by now begun to pursue the arts. Several musical instruments – including flutes made of ivory and of bird bones – have been unearthed in Europe from this and earlier periods. So the art of the campfire sing-song should have been mastered by this time.

At this time, the climate had warmed significantly since the cold days of the Palaeolithic era when humans followed herds of relatively large animals like horses and reindeer. The tundra that covered the country had been replaced by woodland which would have made hunting much more difficult. Meat, such as deer venison, therefore formed a smaller portion of people's diets, while vegetables, berries and roots became more important. It is also clear that people had by now developed a distinct taste for seafood to judge from the bones of salmon, eel, trout and sea bass, and the shells of discarded crabs and crayfish that have been found at old settlements. On the west coast of Scotland vast middens of shellfish detritus have been unearthed by archaeologists. Other finds suggest the menus of the day would have included wild pig, mallard, grouse, wood pigeon, snipe and thrush while diets would have also been augmented by foraging for nuts and berries. Again this is typical of the way hunter-gatherers eke out a living in Africa and Australia today, though the ancient Brits appear to have had their own distinctive ideas about diet. A favourite snack seems to have been roasted hazelnuts. (The chestnut did not arrive until Roman times.) If reindeer meat was the Stone Age Big Mac, hazelnuts were their Pot Noodles.

An example of the power of this hazelnut hunger can be seen on the island of Colonsay, off the west coast of Scotland. In 1994, archaeologist Steven Mithen of Reading University and his students uncovered a 12-foot-wide circular pit – dug around 6,700 BC – that was packed with charred hazelnut shells and other remains, a discovery that

Lesser celandine

turns out to be crucial, not just for revealing details of ancient diets, but in outlining ailments that afflicted our ancestors and the way they treated the environment. 'Nothing like it had ever been found in Scotland,' Mithen says. 'The pit had contained not only burnt fragments of hazelnut shell but also the remnants of apple cores and other plants, especially the lesser celandine.' Lesser celandine is a member of the buttercup family and its roots and stems are still employed by users of traditional medicines who believe the plant has special properties revealed through the plant's alternative name: pilewort. Its purpose is therefore pretty easy to fathom. Certainly, its use suggests at least one unappetising affliction – haemorrhoids – had already become part of the British way of life.

However, the vast scale of Colonsay's hazelnut industry is the real eye-opener. Around the main pit, Mithen and his team found several smaller ones. Hazelnuts were sealed in these, they discovered, and then fires were lit over them. Once roasted, they were gorged by their gatherers and the shells thrown in the main pit. Over the years, these hunter-gatherer visitors stripped Colonsay of its hazel woodland, both for firewood and for nuts. Evidence from ancient pollen found on the island indicates there was an almost complete ecological collapse. 'These hunter-gatherers were certainly not living "in balance" with nature,' Mithen stresses. Today, there are no hazel trees on Colonsay which is ironic given the meaning of the name. 'Coll is the Gaelic word for hazel, so people then must have thought of Colonsay as "hazelnut island",' says Mithen. The destruction of the island's hazel woods shows, if nothing else, what men and women will do if they really want a snack.

In any case, changes were in the offing. Dietary and lifestyle revolutions were about to sweep the country as scientists discovered in 2003 after studying the skeletons of almost 200 ancient Britons. They found that around 4,000 BC, our habit of gorging ourselves on mussels, crabs, prawns, clams and other shellfish, and leaving great middens of discarded shells across the coastline, was abandoned abruptly in favour of diets exclusively made up of meat and cereals. This occurred during the country's transition from the end of the Mesolithic period, when widespread hunter-gatherer activities came to a halt, to the beginning of the Neolithic period which is generally associated with the onset of farming. The discovery of this dietary jump is the work of scientists who exploited a basic fact about the human constitution: that we are what we eat. Mike Richards – who was then based at Bradford University – working with colleagues in Belfast and Oxford, measured isotope ratios in the bones of 164 Neolithic men and women and compared the findings with nineteen fragments of skeletons from Mesolithic people. The method they used exploited the fact that the collagen of our bones is made from proteins derived from our food. These foodstuffs have slightly different isotope signatures depending on whether the proteins come from sea creatures, or the flesh of land mammals, or from crops, or a mixture of all three. To decipher these signatures, the scientists took small pieces of human bone and steeped them in acid to dissolve away unwanted minerals. Then they subjected each to a technique known as mass spectrometry. This allows researchers to measure the ratio of different isotopes of an element in a sample. In the case of the Bradford study, the results provided dramatic details of ancient British diets. Mesolithic people had diets rich in seafood while Neolithic skeletons – whether from coastal or inland sites – showed these people only ate meat and cereals. 'Marine foods, for whatever reason, seem to have been comprehensively abandoned,' states Richards. In short, we moved from 'coquilles St Jacques to lamb and couscous almost overnight', as Tim Radford, writing in the *Guardian*, puts it.

So what, we might reasonably ask, was going on? Why the sudden switch to crops and animal flesh? The answer is, of course, that agriculture had appeared on the scene. The arrival of farming turned our hunter-gatherer ancestors into tillers of the land with a taste for bread and lamb. However, such an explanation does not account for the fact that seafood was dropped completely from diets – which is the really intriguing part of Richards's results. Crabs, crayfish and scallops, some of the most expensive luxury foods today, were removed totally from our ancestors' dinner menus. Accounting for that is not so easy, though Richards has a convincing explanation. Farming did not arrive in dribs and drabs from the other side of the English Channel, he argues. It came as part of a large, cultural package which included beliefs about taboo foods. 'I think they [the hunter-gatherers] fundamentally changed their diet probably immediately when this new material culture arrived,' Richards states. 'It is associated with a package, a whole load of things that appear for the first time in Britain: the first ever pottery, monumental architecture – Stonehenge is the end result of it – and chamber tombs that you bury everyone in. You also for the first time find cereal grains.' These were all linked with the new belief system with the farming of land as its central plank.

This point is backed by Mandy Jay, one of Richards's colleagues. 'We know that the technology for fishing existed and you would have thought that a ready source of food would be exploited,' she says in an interview in the *Independent*. Nevertheless, it was ignored. 'That seems odd from a commonsense point of view. However, it might have been that seafood in some way became taboo. Even now there are dietary taboos – for example, we balk at the thought of eating horsemeat or dog, but these are eaten in some societies.' Surprisingly, this culinary restriction, which shunned the vast supplies of nourishing fish and seafood that would have been available in and around shores, lasted for the next 4,000 years. It took the appearance of the Roman army to knock some dietary sense into the British.

What is clear is that farming did not arrive as a few loose ideas that were taken up by local people so that they gradually spread over the country. The individuals who imported agriculture brought it over as a complete package with a dietary belief system attached for good measure. And those importers clearly knew what they were doing. 'It is becoming clear that farming arrived in a very advanced state 6,000 years ago, after spreading across Europe from the Middle East,' adds Miles. 'These people had mastered all sorts of different ways to exploit the land. Then they set up their operations and farming took off.' This point is supported by Richard Evershed of Bristol University who has developed special techniques for studying fats left in pottery shards that have been

Examination of excavated pottery bowls has revealed that Britons stored animal milk and butter in them

unearthed on these, the first farms of Britain. 'Pots were unglazed then and fats inside them were absorbed into their walls,' he says. 'We took a few bits, crushed them and then analysed them using mass spectrometers. What we found was intriguing. The pots had contained milk – and butter.' In other words, the first British farmers were not people who merely tamed a few animals for subsequent slaughter. They had learned a great deal about the art of good agriculture before they set up their farms and were already experts in the creation of dairy produce. Other studies indicate that they also brought seeds for early forms of wheat and barley and animals such as sheep, a creature which originates in the Middle East.

As to the identity of these first farmers, one only has to look at that Kent longhouse at Blue Bell Hill. The English Channel is only a few miles away, after all. 'This is probably where farming was brought over – from France,' says Miles. Thus both the timing of the construction of White Horse Stone House, and its site, indicates it is a strong candidate to be one of the nation's first farmhouses. Work by Richard Brown and other members of Oxford Archaeology has found the house was probably used only on a seasonal basis, suggesting its occupiers may still have been partly nomadic. It is a slightly confusing picture. A sophisticated farmhouse but occupied by people who still had not quite given up their hunter-gatherer ways. But then some old habits die hard.

Certainly, it is now clear that agriculture was brought to these shores, not by hordes of immigrant farmers but by a limited number of skilled entrepreneurs. 'To read some earlier accounts, one gets the impression that large numbers of people arrived in skin boats, bringing with them the complete DIY kit for setting up a self-sufficient small-holding,' says Francis Pryor. 'They got off the boats, maybe shot a few natives with their new style arrowheads and built themselves substantial houses in which they then lived the Good Life.' In fact, farming's introduction was a much gentler affair and its impact on the people of the time was therefore relatively mild in the sense that it brought no great population changes or alterations to our gene pool. In other ways, however, farming had a considerable effect on the face of Britain. Indeed, it fairly bashed it about to judge from fossil evidence, turning some presumably handsome, well-featured hunter-gatherers into a bunch of pasty-faced, unhealthy misfits. 'In terms of our health and appearance, I don't think there is any doubt that the introduction of farming was bad news for people's health at the time,' says Professor Charlotte Roberts, of Durham University. 'This is true not just of Britain, of course, but of all other parts of the world where people turned their backs on their hunter-gatherer ways and took up the tilling of the land. The result was infectious disease, dental decay, accidental injuries and interpersonal violence.' Roberts, an expert on prehistoric diseases, counsels some caution, however:

> We have plenty of skeletons from the Neolithic period when farming was introduced. And yes, many of them look in poor health. However, we do not have a lot to compare them with, because the period just before that, the Mesolithic, has left us with very few human remains. So we cannot definitely say that farming caused widespread suffering and distress, although fossil evidence from other parts of the world strongly suggests it did.

Consider one study of ancient skeletons from Greece and Turkey mentioned by anthropologist Jared Diamond in his book *The Rise and Fall of the Third Chimpanzee*. 'The average height of hunter-gatherers in that region towards the end of the Ice Age was a generous 5 foot 10 inches for men, 5 foot 6 inches for women,' he says. 'With the adoption of agriculture, height crashed, reaching by 4,000 BC a low value of only 5 foot 3 inches for men, 5 foot 1 inch for women. By classical times, heights were very slowly on the rise again, but modern Greeks and Turks have still not regained the heights of their healthy hunter-gatherer ancestors.' Much the same is true for Britons. We have still to reach the athletic potential of our ancestors.

The reason for this slump in stature is easy to trace, add scientists. We stopped eating a proper diet that had sufficient protein and plumped instead for one low in nutrition and high in calories and carbohydrates. 'We started eating large amounts of cereals,' says Roberts. 'Apart from not giving us a balanced diet, these were high in sugar and low in iron.' The result was widespread dental caries, as can be seen in the riddled teeth of skeletons of Neolithic farmers that have been uncovered by archaeologists. Contrast these with the fine dentures of Cheddar Man that Bryan Sykes so admired when he carried out his mitochondrial analysis of this 9,000-year-old hunter-gatherer and you get a measure of the price we have paid for farming's introduction.

Poor nutrition was only part of the problem, however. For the first time, men and women began to live together in large numbers and were in continual proximity to each other. Huddled in the great sleeping halls of their farming villages, they became ideal breeding grounds for viruses and bacteria. Even worse, these people were also in close contact with their animals and often shared living quarters with them. The result, again noticeable in the fossil record, was the sudden appearance of infections. Just as Asian bird

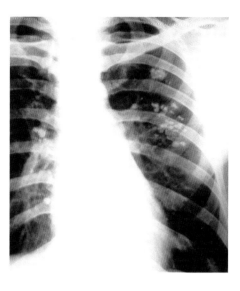

Tuberculosis was common among early farmers

flu is poised to rip through populations today, so microbes – picked up from other creatures – would have occasionally jumped species and triggered local epidemics, often lethal ones. 'We cannot tell exactly what these infections were because skeletal changes could have been caused by many different bacteria,' says Roberts. 'However, there is one exception and that is tuberculosis. It has a striking impact on the human frame if left untreated. It destroys bone and affects hips, knees, and other joints. It also deforms the spine which bends, leaving victims with hunched backs.' Evidence of this illness – which humans probably picked up from cattle – can be seen in Neolithic skeletons.

At the same time, farmers began to develop traumatic wounds and injuries generally absent from the skeletons of their hunter-gatherer ancestors. For males, broken limbs were the main problem and are blamed on Neolithic farmyard accidents. For women, the problem was probably worse. They often ended up spending their days on their knees grinding grain with quern stones. The process would have put intense pressure on their shoulders, elbows, wrists, hips, knees and lower back. The end result: damaged discs and crushed vertebrae. In addition, cartilage between bones became damaged leading to arthritis in joints such as the toes that were constantly pressed down to provide leverage. Another first had been achieved by Stone Age Britons: repetitive strain injuries.

And then there was the final indignity heaped on Neolithic people:

they started fighting each other, or at least the men did. 'On top of everything else we see clear signs of increased interpersonal injuries. In particular, skeletal evidence shows men started to suffer many more head injuries.' Thus the image of a caveman, clubbing rivals and enemies, appears to be a particularly unfair stereotype. It was the farmers who replaced them who seem to have done the fighting, probably over possessions, which for the first time would have begun to play a significant role in everyday lives. Whether or not alcohol was involved, it is difficult to tell. However, people were fermenting drinks by this period, so it is not too fanciful to postulate that the great British cultural export – the pub brawl – may have had its birth in these dim, distant days. In addition, tribal wars over ownership of water access and grazing land appears to have triggered serious turf-wars that killed many people to judge from the appearance of skeletons with arrow injuries. In any case, it was not just our ancestors' stature that suffered dramatically, so did their longevity. 'It is very hard to tell the age at death of an ancient adult human skeleton, but it is quite clear, from a global perspective, that people began to die while they were much younger than they had been in their hunter-gatherer days,' says Roberts. In total, it is a striking collection of ills whose most startling aspect is the number of new ways we found to shorten our lives once we had taken to the life of the farmer.

Given such a list of woes, it is perhaps difficult to understand the success of farming or the reason for its success. The point is that farming enabled many more people to subsist on a piece of land than was possible in the days of the hunter-gatherers. You might have ended up with more aches and pains, and died younger, but you could have many more children and feed them until they matured. We have to some extent cleaned up our act, although there is one feature of farming that still has a major effect on the make-up of Britons today. At some point, just after we had started domesticating animals, we began to drink their milk. It may have been the milk of sheep

Milk has long been central to our diet

that first took our ancestors' fancy. It could even have been that of the reindeer. Either way, they both fell out of favour and cow's milk became the drink of choice, a popularity that remains to this day. Every day, millions of pints are either delivered to homes around Britain or are bought at supermarkets, corner shops and office canteens. More than beer or tea, milk has been the nation's favourite beverage, and although sales have declined a little since their peak in the 1960s, it remains a remarkably popular source of nutrition. Britons love their daily pinta.

But that taste has marked our genes. The problem is that milk consumption beyond infancy is not the norm for mammals. However, for Stone Age farmers, suddenly provided with a new source of sustenance, there would have been new pressures to consume the stuff. Milk is rich in carbohydrate, protein and calcium, after all. The benefits would have seemed obvious from the beginning. 'The problem is that lactose, the key source of carbohydrate in milk, cannot be absorbed by cells,' says Professor Dallas Swallow, of University College, London. 'It has to be broken down into its two components – glucose and galactose – which can then be absorbed and provide nutrition for cells.' The enzyme that is responsible for this breakdown is called lactase. It coats the surfaces of the insides of the small intestine and cracks lactose apart as it passes down the gut, turning it into the precious glucose and galactose. 'The trouble is that in most mammals, and in many people, production of the enzyme lactase is switched off after infancy,' adds Swallow. And when you think about it, that is scarcely surprising. Why should the body make any substance if it is not going to use it any more in life?

As a result, when our hunter-gatherer ancestors, newly introduced to the joys of pastoral life, began to consume animal milk many of them would have got a shock. While other members of their tribe would have swilled the stuff down happily, a Neolithic pint for others would have been a deeply disturbing experience. 'If lactose is not broken down it passes on through the intestines into the colon where it collects and then ferments,' says Swallow. 'You get acids and gas forming in your gut. It can be painful and unpleasant.' Such a condition is known as lactose intolerance and it is acquired by inheriting particular variants of the lactase gene. In such people, the production of lactose is switched off after they are weaned. On average it affects about 5 per cent of the population of the British Isles today. Recent sufferers have included Brooklyn, son of David and Victoria Beckham. The condition is not fatal, it should be stressed, but it can be debilitating and unpleasant and, in Stone Age times, sufferers would have lacked advantages from drinking milk that were being obtained by others. The intriguing point is that lactose intolerance, far from being unusual, was probably the norm for the inhabitants of the British Isles a few thousand years ago. By contrast, lactase persistence – the opposite condition in which adults have no difficulty in consuming animal milk and which is prevalent across most of modern Britain – would have been relatively rare. In other words, there has been a complete switch in our genetic status, thanks to the introduction of farming.

Effectively, those who could not deal with milk, and make the most of its nutritional benefits, would have been at an evolutionary disadvantage. 'The exact nature of this disadvantage is not clear,' adds Swallow. It may be that those who were lactase persistent were just better nourished and so better able to compete for resources and for mates. Milk is rich in calcium, which is good for our bones, for example. Or it could have been that milk at some time in our evolutionary past became the only drink we could have used as an alternative to water, for instance during droughts. 'One of the main symptoms of lactose intolerance is diarrhoea and water loss,' adds Swallow. 'If milk was the only drink available to you and it induced these symptoms, you would have been in serious trouble.'

Drought is not thought to have been a major feature of life in ancient Britain. Such a theory therefore implies that the spread of lactase persistence, and the near extinction of its genetic sibling lactose intolerance evolved somewhere else in Europe, or more probably in the Middle East, the birthplace of farming. 'The trouble is that we have no idea where the trait [of lactase persistence] first arose,' adds Swallow. Certainly, it is strongly associated with agriculture and one would anticipate there would be a gradient of gene intensity beginning with highest levels in the Middle East and in Eastern Europe, and then diminishing the further west you took samples. Yet this is not found when the gene maps of Europe and Britain are consulted. One of the highest levels of lactase persistence, and therefore one of the lowest levels of lactose intolerance, to be found in Europe is in Ireland, just about as far west as you can go in Europe. 'It is a real puzzle why we find that,' admits Swallow. Discovering the distribution of lactase persistence is now a goal being pursued by a number of groups of researchers and should soon produce results that might shed light on the spread of dairy farming through the nation.

In any case, we can now see the kind of impact agriculture had on the nation, at least at a personal level, which, of course, has been our approach in studying the face of Britain. However, we should pause briefly to examine what its introduction meant for the landscape, for this was utterly transformed by farming. The chopping down of the great woodlands that covered the British Isles began at this time, turning a forested countryside into one of hedgerows and fields. And on to this abruptly denuded landscape we then built glorious temples of stone: the rings of Brodgar in Orkney, Callanish in Lewis, Stonehenge in Wiltshire, and other Neolithic wonders. At the same time, we also started building communal tombs and barrows and, later on elaborate burial chambers for rulers and chieftains, as well as great ritual enclosures, or henges as they are known. Indeed, this urge to cover the land with stone appears to have been a powerful one, for it is one of the oddities of farming's arrival that we spent proportionally more time on the Herculean construction of these great edifices than we did on looking after the land, at least in comparison with our Stone Age rivals across the English Channel. 'It is one of the odd features about agriculture in Britain,' says Mark Robinson,

Ancient farming implements such as this plough were used to till the soil

Previous pages:
Stonehenge, one
of our greatest
monuments

of Oxford University. 'We spent much less time working the fields and put all our efforts into building great stone circles and monuments compared to relatives in Europe. We seem to have been obsessed by them.' Certainly, in Britain, the connection between farming, cycles of rebirth and re-growth, and religious experiences was clearly intense to judge from our preoccupation with monumental building. It has also been good for the tourist trade.

Other impacts on the countryside run even deeper as Richard Fortey, senior palaeontologist at the Natural History Museum in London, notes in his book, *Life: An Unauthorised Biography*. As farming spread, he says '. . . sheep and goats became as abundant as people. No longer true fossils, they turn up today when sewage pipes are laid or gardens are deeply dug. They are so common that the Natural History Museum had a special card printed to fend off the enquiries that still come through the door.' In his book, Fortey reprints this card which states, rather charmingly:

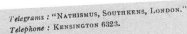

Telegrams : "NATHISMUS, SOUTHKENS, LONDON."
Telephone : KENSINGTON 6323.

BRITISH MUSEUM (NATURAL HISTORY),

CROMWELL ROAD. LONDON, S.W.7.

Dear Sir/Madam,

    The specimen(s) you have submitted for examination is/are a tooth/teeth/bone(s) of horse, cow, pig, sheep or goat, dog.

    The specimen(s) is/are of no great age and is/are not fossil.

            Keeper of Geology.

In fact, the intriguing feature of this list is that every domesticated animal on it was introduced in Neolithic times – with one exception. At excavations at Star Carr, where ancient hunters killed elk, red deer and roe deer for their meat, and pine marten, red fox and beaver for their pelts around 7,500 BC, archaeologists have found signs that these people were already using dogs to help hunt and kill their prey.

The millennia that followed the introduction of farming to Britain arguably represented the most mysterious and intriguing period in the nation's existence, as life in Britain became more complex and as we took greater control of our environment. By around 2,100 BC, the age of stone finally came to an end and Britons turned to metal for their weapons and tools. We opened up mines in Ireland and Wales and mixed tin with copper to make bronze. Farming became more and more intensive and the landscape began to fill with settlements, fields, farms, boundaries and track-ways. At the same time, we returned to our previous fondness for living in roundhouses, as Miles notes: 'You could have any kind of house you liked providing it was round, 8 metres across and had a south-east facing entrance.'

Around this time, or possibly even earlier, Britons began to display urges towards water worship. All sorts of different causeways were built into rivers – including one discovered beside Vauxhall Bridge in central London – and from these a huge array of stone and metal artefacts, human skulls and other bones, have been found. Most were thrown to river gods, it is presumed. This view of water's divine powers was to persist right through Roman times, with a cult centre being built in Bath. Even later, as Miles notes, the monastery at Glastonbury appears to have been placed over an ancient water shrine. 'Even Heathrow airport, I always notice as I rush for a plane, has a pool where travellers cast their coins,' he adds. 'Clearly water has made a deep impression on the British people.'

At the same time, there were undoubted large movements of individual groups and families in and out of the British Isles, but as far as scientists and historians can tell from the archaeological record, there were no major influxes or immigrations of foreigners to upset the nation's gene pool.

Then, around 450 BC, the Iron Age replaced the Bronze Age, with Britons learning how to handle an altogether trickier but hardier metal. At this time, the nation's first great tribal kingdoms were born and the first coins also appear in archaeological records. Life got more and more sophisticated, though the days when Britons were free to run this exciting new world for themselves were numbered. In 55 BC and 54 BC, Julius Caesar launched two fairly disastrous attempts to 'persuade' the British to stop providing support for the Gauls who were then harassing his legions.

The Romans built
Hadrian's Wall to
defend the northern
boundaries of their
empire

The Romans returned in proper numbers in AD 43 and conquered southern Britain where they held sway for almost 400 years. The city of London was created, Hadrian's Wall built to mark the colony's northern extreme, and grand villas and temples constructed. Yet it is clear that few Romans came to live in Britain and instead relied on legions recruited initially from northern Europe, and then later some from Britain itself, to control affairs. Again, little was added to the nation's gene pool and the bloodline of the British people was left untouched by major population movements. Indeed life under the Romans appears to have been a rather domesticated business. From the evidence of letters – which were then written on thin wooden tablets – found at Vindolanda, which later became one of the forts on Hadrian's Wall, archaeologists have discovered communications then largely involved requests for leave, complaints about impassable roads, and lists of foodstuffs. One letter, clearly from a worried mum, concerned about her son's posting to the cold and hostile north states: 'I have sent you some socks, two pairs of sandals and two pairs of underpants. I hope you are getting on with your messmates.' Some things never change.

As to the question of what the Romans did for Britain, the answer is clearly that they did a lot. Studies of skeletons in Iron Age and Roman graves indicate that there was a significant drop in the death rate and a leap in population growth. Roman towns had relatively good water supplies and sanitary facilities and Britons prospered. As Miles points out:

> For much of the [Roman] period, improved long-distance and local transport, an international currency, intervals of peace, increased agricultural productivity, improved water supply, and a modicum of public health led to an increasing population until the late 4th century. By then, however, Roman Britain was in trouble. Across Europe the empire was in a state of military and economic collapse. Coinage dried up, wages went unpaid, industries collapsed, towns decayed, villas fell into a state of disuse, ditches were no longer cleared. Roman Britain was in a state of crisis; the barbarians were at the door.

In AD 410, the Roman legions finally withdrew. Britons, who were now largely untutored in martial skills, were left exposed to the predations of tribes of Picts and Scots to the north. So the leaders of the kingdoms that had sprung up in the wake of the Romans appealed to the leaders of the Anglo-Saxon peoples across the North Sea in Friesland and Saxony for help. This was an unwise move, as we shall see.

CHAPTER FIVE

Word Power

*The country was now almost entirely inhabited by
Saxons and was therefore named England, and thus
(naturally) soon became C. of E. This was a Good Thing,
because previously the Saxons had worshipped some
dreadful gods of their own called Monday, Tuesday,
Wednesday, Thursday, Friday and Saturday.*

W.C. SELLAR AND R.J. YEATMAN, *1066 AND ALL THAT*

I t would be a mammoth – if not impossible – task to list the
achievements of the people of the British Isles. Their influence, both
for good and for bad, on global affairs has been formidable. Just
consider this sample list: the discovery of penicillin; the building, during
the Boer War, of the first concentration camps; the launching of the
Industrial Revolution; the development of the armoured tank; and the
inventions of television, computers, anaesthetics, genetic fingerprinting,
and radar. Then there is the country's role in creating the current forms
of football, rugby, tennis, golf, and cricket while the world can also thank
us for sandwiches, Christmas cards, Boy Scouts, stamps, and – thanks to
Mary Shelley – science fiction novels. On top of this, come the works of
Darwin, the Beatles, Newton, Burns, Brunel, Chaplin, Turner,
McGonagall, Hitchcock, Joyce and, of course, Shakespeare.

You may love or loathe the people of the British Isles but you cannot
disregard their impact. They have simply been too busy to be ignored, a
point most vividly demonstrated by the English language, the nation's

*What the British
gave the world:
stamps, William
Shakespeare, the
Christmas card
and the Beatles*

109

greatest legacy of all. Today well over a billion people speak English and given that it is now the world's most frequently taught second language, these figures are destined to rise significantly. More people may utter words in Chinese on a daily basis but you can be sure English speakers have a greater international impact, a point stressed by Jeremy Paxman in his book *The English: A Portrait of a People*:

> When an Icelander meets a Peruvian, each reaches for his English. Even in the Second World War, when the foundations were being laid for the Axis pact between Germany, Japan and Italy, Yosuke Matsuoka was negotiating for the emperor in English. It is the medium of technology, science, travel, and international politics. Three-quarters of the world's mail is written in English, four-fifths of all data stored on computers is in English, and the language is used by two-thirds of the world's scientists. It is easy to learn, very easy to speak badly; a little learning will take you quite a long way, which is why an estimated one quarter of the entire world population can speak the language to some degree.

Of course, the popularity of the language has a lot to do with the influence of America. The single, largest group of native speakers live in the United States and their enthusiasm for Internet-driven dialogue ensures English is being channelled into millions of new households around the world each year. Not that the potential of this transatlantic influence was lost on previous generations. 'The most important element in modern history is the fact that the North Americans speak English,' Bismarck remarked presciently more than a century ago. Thus we can see that for a long time English has been a '. . . world language-in-waiting which conquered America, and was primed by the industrial revolution and the growth of empires here and across the Atlantic by technology and mass communication,' writes Melvyn Bragg, author of *The Adventure of English: The Biography of a Language*.

It is not just a matter of international politics, however. English has its own intrinsic qualities. It is highly adaptable, logical in composition (with some exceptions), and blessed with a mighty lexicon of nouns, adjectives and phrases that continually evolve. Above all, English is malleable and fluid, a flexibility generally enjoyed by most speakers as is demonstrated, every year, with the publication of fresh editions of a Collins or an Oxford dictionary. These events are greeted in the British press with a barrage of articles about that year's new entries. A few conservatives carp about vulgar newcomers but overall most commentators welcome these linguistic arrivistes. In recent years, these have included bling-bling, chav, chugger, getting asboed, podcast, pear-shaped, spinmeister, and multi-task. To the French, such additions would be an anathema and its authorities wage a constant war on unwelcome interloping phrases and nouns. English speakers have no such problems and generally relish their presence, as well as the contradictions that sometimes ensue. As the American humourist Franklin Jones once affectionately remarked: 'It's a strange world of languages, in which skating on thin ice can get you into hot water.' Or as Gustav White pointed out: 'Our language is funny – a fat chance and a slim chance are the same thing.' In this rather haphazard way the English language has expressed the thoughts of generations.

But if this was Britain's greatest gift to the world, who gave it to us in the first place? Who first stood on our shores, uttering words that we might recognise as the English language today? And where and when? These questions, it transpires, have profound implications for our searches into the history of the British people. Short-term answers to them are surprisingly straightforward, however. For a start, the place and date of this momentous linguistic event can be pinned to the coast of eastern England in the early fifth century, probably around AD 420. As to the identity of its speakers, we know quite clearly who first uttered words in proto-English in the British Isles. They were people from a region we now call Friesland, in northern Holland, and lands to the east and north, including Saxony, in what is western Germany today. We call them the Saxons, the Angles and the Jutes – though we now tend to clump them together under the heading of Anglo-Saxons. These individuals spoke an Indo-European language of a Germanic subtype, the linguistic category in which English is now classed. Of course, English has changed a lot over the centuries. In the eleventh century, the Normans introduced hundreds of French words, for example, and since then there has been a constant trickle of new nouns, verbs and phrases from an array of different sources including India, the West Indies and

Anglo-Saxons wore circular brooches like this one

America. Nevertheless, modern English is still based on the Anglo-Saxon language spoken by those immigrants 1,500 years ago.

This point was neatly demonstrated in 2006, when the Oxford University Press published the nouns most used by the average person. 'Time' turned out to be the commonest, followed by 'person', then 'year', then 'way', and then 'day'. Others in the top 20 include 'man' (7th), 'child' (12th) and 'woman' (14th) as well as 'hand' (10th), 'part' (11th), and 'eye' (13th). The common denominators for these words are their brevity, and their origin – Anglo-Saxon. Even today, we can have long conversations in the Old English that the Anglo-Saxons brought over. Just consider these words, from one of the most famous passages in British history. 'We shall fight on the beaches, we shall fight on the landing grounds, we shall fight in the fields and in the streets, we shall fight in the hills; we shall never surrender.' These are the ringing phrases of Winston Churchill, speaking in 1940, in defiance of Nazi Germany. The key point is that every single word he used in that magnificent piece of oratory is Old English – with one exception, as Bragg points out. 'Only surrender is not Old English. That, in itself, might be significant.' And if you visit Friesland today, you will be struck by the similarity, both in spellings of words and their pronunciations. There is 'see' (sea), 'buter' (butter), 'rein' (rain), 'boat' (boat) 'brea' (bread) and 'sliepe' (sleep), for example. As Bragg makes clear: Friesian was a strong parent of English.

Clearly, the tongue of the Anglo-Saxons has come a long way and since been transformed into a twenty-first century linguistic leviathan spoken and understood by between one and two billion people. Those strangers on the shores of Kent and Essex have had an extraordinary influence. But if their impact on our language was so considerable, what was their effect on the population of the British Isles? How were the men and women who lived in post-Roman Britain affected by the arrival of the people of Friesland and Saxony? What sort of changes were made to the British bloodline? These questions are far trickier to answer, it transpires. Indeed, they lead us into the most contentious of all issues concerning the peopling of the British Isles, a debate that still causes intense disagreement among historians and archaeologists. At its heart, the issue is simple. Some say the Anglo-Saxons arrived in Britain in waves and overwhelmed the tattered remnants of Romano-British people. Others argue that their impact was a relatively benign one involving a few warrior bands gaining control of British regional kingdoms from which they encouraged the exchange of ideas and goods. Scholars and scientists are still bitterly divided between these two camps and in their interpretations of events during this dark, romantic period when the nation was 'a no-man's land, across which flit insubstantial, semi-legendary figures – Hengist and Horsa, Arthur, Alfred and Offa', as the archaeologist David Wilson puts it in *The Anglo-Saxons*. The difference between these two schools is not just a matter of scholarly dispute. The manner of the Anglo-Saxons' arrival in the British Isles is crucial to our story because these people may be the one group of individuals to have made profound changes to the British gene-pool that had been established thousands of years earlier. Given that this academic battle is so important to our story, we should pause briefly to examine the claims.

For many years, the invasion scenario was considered to be an unshakeable account of our past. The Anglo-Saxons – the men carrying circular wooden shields with central iron bosses, and the women wearing saucer brooches and amber beads – swept over the North Sea in flotillas of boats and took over the southern and eastern parts of the country, filling a void left by the Romans. They poured into central England and pushed the natives westward into Wales and south-west England. These corners became the last bastions of ancient British culture. The rest of England became Anglo-Saxon. Towns were abandoned

Helmet from the Anglo-Saxon Sutton Hoo ship burial

and most of the population reverted to life in the countryside and small villages. On top of this, an entirely new range of day-to-day objects appeared in Britain – pottery, brooches, axes and knives – as well as a new pagan religion and a new way of dealing with the dead: cremation. At the same time, houses were built with sunken floors or cellars for the first time while long, rectangular hall-like buildings appeared in villages.

As for evidence, you only have to look at the way that Old English terms have penetrated every aspect of British life, say invasion supporters. Even the days of the week were altered to commemorate the Anglo-Saxon gods of Tiw, Woden and Thor while the goddess Eostere's name was retained for the Christian festival of Easter. In addition there are the words 'spinster' and 'wif-man', a weaving person, from which comes the modern English word 'wife'. They also gave the British Isles the name of one of its countries – England, the land of the Angles – as well as the idea

Anglo-Saxon invasions of Britain

of class-consciousness which emerged from the Anglo-Saxons' strict laws of social ranking. By contrast, only a couple of dozen ancient British words remain in use today, mainly ones that describe landscape features such as 'crag' or 'lake'. Only a complete conquest can account for a linguistic and cultural impact of this magnitude, it is argued. A handful of individuals popping over to set up businesses in Britain would have brought few alterations to life in Britain. We would still be speaking Celtic languages, or Latin, or an amalgam of the two if that had been the case. Our current talk 'of the ways of men' and 'the time of day' would have been restricted to a few whelk-sellers plying their trade on the east coast of England. The key changes had to be imposed physically on unwilling natives by large numbers of immigrants – with corresponding implications for the land's gene-pool.

For further support, invasion supporters point to the records of the clerics Gildas and Bede, writing in the sixth and seventh centuries respectively. Bede describes a country succumbing to slaughter and attacks from Picts and Scots after the departure of the Romans. The British people appealed to Rome, says Bede. 'To Aetius, Consul, come the groans of the Britons … The barbarians drive us into the sea, and the sea drives us back to the barbarians. Between these, two deadly alternatives confront us, drowning or slaughter.' The Romans had their own problems, of course, so the ancient Britons of the South – who were now fairly defenceless – turned for help to the Anglo-Saxons. These German tribes often acted as mercenaries at this time so the Romano-Britons hired them to fight off the raiders. Thus it was decided, according to Gildas, that 'the ferocious Saxons (name not to be spoken!) hated by man and God should be let into the island like wolves into the fold, to beat the peoples of the north … a pack of cubs burst forth like the lair of the barbarian lioness, coming in three keels, as they call warships in their language'. In this way, the Anglo-Saxons arrived in their ships, liked what they saw, and conquered it. It was a straight military conquest.

This idea has recently come under attack, however. 'Many scholars argue there was no significant change in population,' says David Miles. 'The natives, influenced by an Anglo-Saxon military elite, simply adopted the clothing, jewellery, language, and religion of their rulers.' To these archaeologists and historians, the evidence for the conquering of Britain by people from Friesland and Saxony is non-existent, a point stressed by Francis Pryor in his book, *Britain AD*. 'What caused a supposedly near collapse in southern British elite and military circles in little more than a generation? If such a thing did happen, one would expect it to have left clear archaeological traces: massive war graves, settlement dislocation and "knock-on" impacts in northern and western Britain. But so far they have not been found.' If waves of Anglo-Saxons subjugated the ancient British and introduced their fancy new practices, you would anticipate finding distinctions between the practices of the new elite and enslaved natives. 'One would expect to find distinct "Anglo-Saxon" and British cemeteries close to the same settlements, but that does not happen', adds Pryor. 'There is precious little evidence for a fifth century elite of any sort, let alone a foreign one.'

Yes, some warrior bands took over a few local kingdoms but there were no conquering armies. Anglo-Saxon practices and culture were adopted because people changed their minds not their places of residence. According to Pryor it is 'probably fair to say that serious scholars who believe in large-scale Anglo-Saxon mass migrations are now in the minority.' As he points out, if the invasion theory is correct, then up to a million people from the eastern and central parts of England would have been driven from their homes and would have been sent streaming away from advancing Anglo-Saxon armies. To date, we have found no archaeological traces of such an exodus, he says. This is why Pryor backs the idea that a fairly limited military elite took over the small kingdoms that peppered southern Britain. Then its commanders enticed Saxon tradesmen and artisans to follow in their wake and to introduce new practices to the country. This kind of Anglo-Saxon 'invasion' involves a process known as acculturation which is defined by Timothy Darvill, in the *Oxford Dictionary of Archaeology*, as 'transference of ideas, beliefs and traditions . . . by long-term personal contact and interaction between communities or societies. Adoption through assimilation by prolonged contact.' In other words, there was no occupation by ravaging pagan furies but a slow and steady influx of immigrants who brought over new crops, new ways to farm and new tools for working the land. This would have had only a modest impact on the British gene pool. The ideas of the Anglo-Saxons travelled, not their genes. An abrupt transition from

Roman power to total Anglo-Saxon military control is also dismissed by Simon Schama in his *A History of Britain*. As he says, the governing institutions of the Roman province did fall away. 'But much of the social practices and culture and even the language of the old Britain persisted long after the arrival of the first few bands of Saxon mercenaries and freebooters. For many generations, Roman-Britons and North Sea warriors must have lived alongside each other, as neighbours rather than implacable foes.'

We should note that the difference between the two camps goes to the heart of our understanding of what it means to be British, for it had been assumed for a long time that a large input of Anglo-Saxon genes was crucial to defining the English people. At the same time, these invaders were also implicated in the fate of the ancient Britons who – pushed into their western and northern bolt holes – would have joined the founders of the Cornish, Welsh, Irish and Scottish people. Now a group of historians and archaeologists have started to claim that this army did not really exist, at least as a significant wave of attackers. The position is summed up by Pryor: 'If we are looking for English origins, we should forget the "Anglo-Saxons" and turn instead to the resident population, who had been there, in their millions, and in their various cultures and communities all the time.' It is a fairly stark view. But who is correct? Was it military might that brought Saxon ways to Britain or a relatively, gentle cultural infusion? It is a fairly profound set of issues to differ over, it has to be admitted. Fortunately these concerns are ideally suited to the analytical power of genetics, as we have already noted in Chapter Two. There we learned how Walter Bodmer's People of the British Isles project had pinpointed signs – in the form of red-hair genes and other variants – of the presence of ancient British blood in the land's 'Celtic' corners: Cornwall, Wales, Scotland and Ireland. We also examined the reasons for these concentrations of 'Celtic' genes and indicated that a population push from the east by the Anglo-Saxons was probably involved. So let us now examine, in greater detail, how geneticists are helping to uncover the true influence of the Anglo-Saxons on the British population.

One of the first attempts to study Anglo-Saxon genes was made by an international team of scientists from University College, London, the University of California, Davis, and Vrije Universiteit, Amsterdam.

They decided to examine the Y-chromosomes of men at various points along a slice of English countryside that runs east–west from the coast of Norfolk to Anglesey, in Wales. Seven ancient market towns, each mentioned in the Domesday Book and separated from the next by a distance of around 30 miles, were picked as sampling points. Starting from the east, and moving west, they are: North Walsham, Fakenham, Bourne, Southwell, and Ashbourne, in England, and Abergele and Llangefni in Wales. Each is small, with a population of between 5,000 and 10,000 and was not thought likely to have been affected by significant migrations in recent years.

The scientists then took spittle samples from local men whose fathers and paternal grandfathers had been born within 15 miles of these towns. A total of 313 men were tested this way. In addition, the researchers took samples from 94 men from Friesland. Then they set about analysing the Y-chromosomes of their volunteers. The results were dramatic. First, the researchers found there was little genetic difference between the men of the five English towns. Second, they found no difference between the samples from these towns and from Friesland. And third, they found the two Welsh towns were markedly different from both those of England or Friesland. 'Our results indicate the presence of a strong genetic barrier between Central England and North Wales and the virtual absence of a barrier between central England and Friesland,' they state in a paper published in *Molecular Biology and Evolution*. Or as Mark Thomas, one of the UCL members of the team, puts it: 'The English are more like Friesians than they are like the Welsh.'

According to this study, we can clearly see the tell-tale signs of a violent Anglo-Saxon takeover in the blood and the tissue of the men of the market towns of England and Wales. This data indicates there was a near complete replacement in east and central England of between 50 to 100 per cent of the male gene pool by men from Friesland and Saxony. Such figures speak of martial conquest and genocide in the English countryside and certainly offers little support for supporters of the non-invasion school. The gene study also endorses the notion that ancient British people successfully lived in Wales defying the armies of the Anglo-Saxons. For the next seven or eight hundred years, the Welsh fought with the English. At one point, Offa, the king of Mercia – whose compressed likeness on a coin was encountered in Chapter One – built a 150-mile-long barrier, Offa's Dyke, to keep out the Welsh and the two sides remained linguistically, culturally and politically separate until 1282 when Edward I of England defeated the Welsh King Llywelyn II. Even then, there was little interaction, according to the study. 'Our results suggest that this separation has restricted male-mediated gene flow between the two regions over the past approximately 1,500 years.' In other words, when it came to mating, the Welsh and the Anglo-Saxons have had little to do with each other for more than a millennium. As the scientists conclude: 'This study shows that the Welsh border was more of a genetic barrier to Anglo-Saxon Y-chromosome gene flow than the North Sea.'

Edward I, who defeated Llywelyn

It was a fairly stark set of results and certainly gave a boost to the invasion school's flagging fortunes. Their opponents did not have to wait long for a chance to fight back, however. A separate study was launched by a group led by David Goldstein who is also based at University College London. Goldstein's team created a grid which they placed over the map of the British Isles and used as the basis for a massive sampling of Y-chromosomes. A total of 1,772 men took part in the study, living in twenty-five towns space evenly across the British Isles ranging from those who lived in Shetland, Orkney and Durness on the very north coast of Scotland, to Pitlochery and Oban, further south, to Penrith and Morpeth in northern England, and to Faversham and Dorchester in the very south. Other sites in Wales, Cornwall and Ireland were also selected, as well as groups of men from Denmark, Norway and Germany. This time, a very different set of results were produced. For a start, the transition between Wales and England – which the previous group of researchers had found to be clear and well-delineated appeared to be a gradual affair according to Goldstein's DNA analysis.

That was surprising enough. But there was more to follow. According to the researchers led by Goldstein, the most startling conclusion 'is the limited continental input in southern England which appears to be predominantly indigenous and by some analyses, no more influenced by continental invaders than is mainland Scotland [a part of the country generally thought to be free of such incursions]'. In other words, there were only relatively modest signs of the presence of Anglo-Saxon genes – at least, those on the Y-chromosome – in southern England, despite expectations of a major contribution. At the same time, evidence of a major Anglo-Saxon incursion from the east, ending abruptly at the Welsh border, was not found. This time it was the non-invasion school that got the good news, leaving the battle between the two camps finely balanced. And that leads us neatly to the next phase of Walter Bodmer's People of the British Isles study. What would he make of the great Anglo-Saxon question? Crucially Bodmer's approach to the study of the British people employs the use of a host of different genetic variants, including those concerned with rhesus negativity, as well as biological markers of the HLA system, which – as we saw in Chapter Two – are used by cells to demonstrate they are not foreign bodies when they encounter the body's immune cells. It is not limited to the single set of Y-chromosome markers used by Mark Thomas and his collaborators or by David Goldstein and his team.

In fact, Bodmer's technique makes it possible to put a value to an individual's prospect of being a Celt or an Anglo-Saxon. You can say a person is 7.3 times more likely to be an Anglo-Saxon than a Celt, or that he or she is 9 times more likely to be a Celt than an Anglo-Saxon according to his methodology. It is the first time that a scientist has ever been able to ascribe such a loading to an individual's British roots and is one of the most exciting aspects of the People of the British Isles project. Bodmer achieves this by basing his analysis on two of the main ancestral types that make up the British people, the Anglo-Saxons and the Celts, or to be more precise the ancient Britons. The people rated by Bodmer as being most like the ancient Britons are those from Cornwall because this is where these people are most likely to have ended up, pressed into south-west England as far from the Anglo-Saxons as they can get, he argues. By contrast, Bodmer assumes the people most like to be Anglo-Saxon in origin are those from East Anglia and Lincolnshire, the first places to have born the brunt of those waves of incoming Saxons.

These two distinct profiles – one based on those of the people of Cornwall and Devon and the other on the people of East Anglia and Lincolnshire – represent opposite ends of a genetic spectrum.

'Essentially, we take a look at a specific range of factors – blood group, whether a person is rhesus negative or positive, which variants of five genes, related to tissue matching and transplantation, that an individual possesses, and the versions of the MC1R gene that we find in their DNA,' says Bruce Winney, the project's manager. 'When we find out what a person's particular genetic profile is for these variants, we calculate what the probability is of a Celtic person having that profile and what is the chance that an Anglo-Saxon will have one like it. Then we divide which ever turns out to be the smaller of the two numbers into the larger.

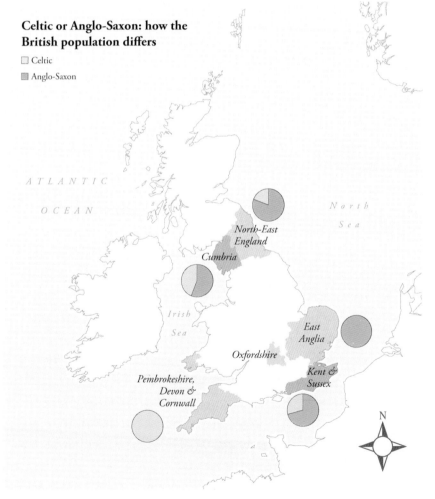

Celtic or Anglo-Saxon: how the British population differs

☐ Celtic
▦ Anglo-Saxon

How Britain's Celtic and Anglo-Saxon heritage varies, according to Bodmer: from full Celtic ancestry in Cornwall to complete Anglo-Saxon ancestry in East Anglia. People from counties in between are a mixture depending on the histories of the occupations of their homeland.

In that way, we end up with a figure which indicates whether a person is more likely to be Anglo-Saxon or Celtic.' For those taking part in the People of the British Isles project, statistics like these were awaited with great anticipation.

Some volunteers may have sought confirmation of Anglo-Saxon roots, but most desired a very different outcome. 'When it came to their roots, most people wanted either to be Celtic or Viking,' says Winney. 'Being Anglo-Saxon was definitely third on the list.' A classic example is provided by Jack Graham, a retired draughtsman, who lives in Rowlands Gill in the Tyne and Wear region. He volunteered for the People of the

Great Danes

Gordon Dane is the seventy-four-year-old director of the Faversham Oyster Fishery, one of most ancient companies in the British Isles. His father was a fishermen, as was his father's father, as was his father's father's father. At the same time, the name Dane appears on street names, parks and farms throughout the countryside that surrounds his home town of Faversham on the north Kent coast. Dane considers himself to be an Anglo-Saxon to his roots. 'We were the rough and ready sort, like the other Anglo-Saxons, the fishermen and farmers of England,' he says. And to his considerable pleasure, Gordon found his genetic profile strongly backed such an origin. His blood group was A, with a rhesus negative factor, while his HLA cells were relatively rare for the nation but relatively common in Kent and Sussex. This combination allowed Bodmer to assess Gordon's ancestry as being 6.4 times more likely to belong to an Anglo-Saxon than a Celt, and 14 times more likely to be from Sussex and Kent than from the Celtic fringe. 'I am very happy with that,' says Gordon. 'That is just how I see myself – a true-bred Anglo-Saxon.'

British Isles project because he, like other blood donors, was fascinated with his genealogy and local history. 'Really, I had hoped it would be found I would have Viking blood,' he says. 'Vikings were quite common in this part of the world. But it didn't turn out that way.' Instead, Bodmer found Jack was 7.4 times more likely to be an Anglo-Saxon than a Celt, an origin that can be traced to his great-grandfather Jeremiah Graham. 'The story is that he originally came from East Anglia,' says Jack. 'In those days the ships that carried coal from Newcastle to London called in on ports in Norfolk on their way back to the Tyne. They had recruiting officers for the pits on board and they would get local lads to sign up to become miners. They got Jeremiah that way. One week he was in the cornfields of East Anglia, the next he was down the coal mines. It wouldn't have been pleasant. When it came to my turn to go down the pits when I left school, my father decided there had been enough members of the family who had been miners and he arranged for me to get an engineering apprenticeship. So I never had to go down the mines.'

Then there is Non Torries – whom we encountered in Chapter Two and who believed her Welshness defined her. She was also very keen to find evidence that her origins were not Anglo-Saxon. She, of course, wanted to be a Celt. The question was: would the project confirm those roots? This time the answer was yes, however. Non's blood group was B negative while her HLA Class II combination of 03-02 turns out to be more common in Wales than the rest of the country. According to Bodmer, Non is 1.4 times more likely to be a Celt than an Anglo-Saxon and eight times more likely to be from Wales than from the non-Celtic fringe. 'The result could not have been better,' she says. 'I was delighted. I know I am Celtic and Welsh but it is good to have something like this, which you feel is so deeply, confirmed by science.'

And the same goes for Ken Sweet – who we also met in Chapter Two and who is descended from a long line of Cornish miners. He was delighted with his results which also revealed his Celtic origins. According to Bodmer's rating he is 1.9 times more likely to be a Celt than an Anglo-Saxon. 'I am absolutely thrilled. It was good to have it confirmed that I am a Cornish man. As far as I can see my ancestors could have been among the very first people who came to Britain when it was still attached by land to Europe. I think that makes us very special people and shows why my family feels such a bond with Cornwall.'

Bodmer was also able to survey various English counties and ascribe for each a ratio of their Celtic genes against their Anglo-Saxon genes. (These analyses assume, of course, that Cornwall, Devon and Wales are the most Celtic parts of southern Britain and that East Anglia and Lincolnshire are the most Anglo-Saxon.) The results were intriguing. In the north-east of England, made up of the counties of Northumberland and Durham, the bias was definitely Anglo-Saxon: 77 per cent against only 23 per cent Celtic. This figure was even stronger than for Sussex and Kent which were only 71 per cent Anglo-Saxon as opposed to 29 per cent Celtic. For its part, Cumbria was 44 per cent Celtic as opposed to 56 per cent Anglo-Saxon. However the real surprise came in Oxfordshire which turns out to be slightly more Celtic than Anglo-Saxon, 51 per cent against 49. This last figure is undoubtedly an unexpected one, if you assume the Anglo-Saxons took over the heart of England. Oxfordshire and the upper Thames valley are areas where there was an almost complete replacement of older settlements with those of the Anglo-Saxons. You can see the effects today. Celtic place names have almost

Widdecombe's Way

Tory MP Ann Widdecombe has a distinctive, rare name. There were less than a hundred Widdecombes in the Electoral Register for 1998, while results from the 1881 census shows a tight cluster of people with the surname in Devon. 'I had always expected to have Celtic roots,' she says. 'My family history suggests that. There is even talk that there was a Cornish wrecker in the family somewhere.' It was not to be, however. Bodmer's results shows that the MP's ancestry was more or less 50 per cent Anglo-Saxon and 50 per cent Celtic. Widdecombe is phlegmatic, nevertheless 'I have no problem with that,' she says, 'I am proud to be both Celtic and Anglo-Saxon.'

completely disappeared from the landscape. The Thames is one of the few Celtic names left in the area. Certainly, Bodmer's analyses do not show the results you would expect if middle England had been completely overwhelmed by Anglo-Saxons.

The issue is still unresolved, though from the studies of Bodmer and Goldstein, it is clear there is a fair amount of evidence to support the idea of Anglo-Saxon acculturation as opposed to invasion. Certainly these two sets of findings do not sit easily beside those of Thomas and his team. However, some attempts at a compromise have been made by various historians and scientists. One intriguing idea, backed by the Oxford historian Mark Robinson, suggests there may have been considerable depopulation after the departure of the Romans so that Anglo-Saxons poured into an empty landscape. This might account for the genetic confusion. 'There is evidence that suggests a huge void in the population – caused by an as yet unknown epidemic of disease – appeared in southern Britain at this time,' Robinson says. This view is backed by Miles. 'At some point in the middle of the 5th century there seems to have been an enormous collapse in the population. We don't know why. Possibly the plague was involved though we have found no plague pits into which bodies were thrown. Something triggered a substantial population drop, however.' Thus the North Sea newcomers arrived in a land of emptied towns and fields and so repopulated the land without recourse to killings or the seizure of land or property. And as Miles notes in *The Tribes of Britain*, the population of Britain – which is estimated to have been around 3 million during the heyday of the Romans – probably plummeted to half that number by the time the Anglo-Saxons arrived. Thus the men and women of Friesland and Saxony simply made the most of an opportunity to better themselves and increase their numbers.

Another – even more controversial – suggestion has been put forward by Thomas himself in a paper in the Proceedings of the Royal Society in 2006. As he acknowledges, he and his colleagues – after they published their original results in 2002 – came in for a fairly sustained assault from archaeologists and other scholars on the grounds of lack of supporting evidence. So Thomas went back to his computer, and keyed in a number of different scenarios in a bid to explain their market town results. Eventually, he came up with an alternative model – and it turned out to be a corker. Yes, you could find a way to get round the involvement of waves of immigrants and invaders and still account for the prevalence of Friesian genes in our midst, said Thomas – but only if you accepted that the Anglo-Saxons kept control of their newly subjugated lands by introducing a policy of strict segregation, one that allowed the newcomers to outbreed the ancient British natives. 'Essentially they operated a system very like the apartheid regime that was set up in South Africa last century,' says Mark Thomas.

This notion avoids the lack of archaeological evidence for huge numbers of invaders and immigrants whose 'existence' was originally implied by Thomas and his colleagues. It is not merely a back-of-an-envelope calculation aimed at avoiding inconvenient facts, however. As Thomas stresses the idea of an Anglo-Saxon apartheid is based on historical evidence. For example, texts such as the Laws of Ine indicate the lives of the incomers were treated as being far more precious and important than those of native Britons. According to Thomas:

> Essentially, the native Britons were genetically and culturally absorbed by the Anglo-Saxons over a period of as little as a few hundred years. An initially small invading Anglo-Saxon elite could have quickly established themselves by having more children who survived to adulthood, thanks to their military power and economic advantage. We believe that they also prevented the native British genes getting into the Anglo-Saxon population by restricting intermarriage in a system of apartheid that left the country culturally and genetically Germanised.

It is an intriguing argument though it remains to be seen how archaeologists and historians of the non-invasion school respond. At present, there is evidence to back either side. Indeed it is a mystery why the various groups have produced studies that have such wildly differing implications for the history of the Anglo-Saxon period. Differences in methodology, including variations in sample size, the personal histories of participants, and the numbers of different gene markers used by the researchers will all have a profound impact on results. Most probably, the truth lies somewhere in the middle of the two scenarios that are outlined by supporters of the two camps, as Bodmer acknowledges. 'I think that the two extremes are probably both wrong,' he says. 'It was most likely that soldiers came over, stayed and proved to be very successful at farming. They bred more, as a result.'

The jury is still out on the issue, nevertheless. Suffice to say the Anglo-Saxons remain our most mysterious visitors, though – to be fair – it would seem that the genetic evidence does not favour the idea of genocide and a mass takeover of the nation and suggests that something slightly subtler went on. On the other hand, it is equally clear the Anglo-Saxons had a substantial impact on our population and in some parts of southern Britain, they account for up to 50 per cent of local gene pools.

In any case, even if we cannot yet decide definitively if the Anglo-Saxons arrived with war on their minds or trade, we have no such worries with the next set of visitors to our shores. They came to Britain with violent and larcenous intentions and never shirked from implementing them.

CHAPTER SIX

Hammer of the Gods

Never before has such terror appeared in Britain as we have now suffered from a pagan race ... Behold, the church of St. Cuthbert, spattered with the blood of the priests of God, despoiled of all its ornaments; a place more venerable than all in Britain is given as a prey to pagan peoples.
ALCUIN OF YORK IN A LATE EIGHTH-CENTURY LETTER TO
ETHELRED, KING OF NORTHUMBRIA IN ENGLAND

The rolling hills that stretch across the central belt of main island Orkney are famed for their bleak and windswept aspect. There is an austere beauty to this landscape, though few would claim it to be exquisite or lovely – except archaeologists. To them, the Orkney countryside is more appealing, and far richer, than most other areas of Britain – and for a very basic reason: it positively bristles with ancient settlements, stone rings and tombs. There are eight of these wonders on average on each square mile of Orkney soil. For anyone interested in British prehistory, these islands are a magnet.

There is the village of Skara Brae on the west coast, a huddle of now roofless houses built by Neolithic fishermen and farmers; the nearby Ring of Brodgar, one of Britain's finest stone circles; and the Standing Stones of Stenness, the petrified bodies of drunken giants according to local legend.

The Ring of Brodgar standing stones in the Orkney Islands, Scotland

All are striking edifices. However, if you want to try to understand the immense timescale of human activity on this 'sculptural, wind-honed archipelago' – as the Scottish poet Kathleen Jamie describes Orkney – then prime place goes to the chambered cairn of Maes Howe, a vast communal grave built more than 4,000 years ago.

From the outside, the tomb is unspectacular. It appears as no more than a large grassy knoll in a field beside the main road between Orkney's two main towns, Kirkwall and Stromness. Things are different inside, however. You pass through a low, 25-foot-long passageway, half-crouching, half-crawling, into a high sandstone-clad vault. 'You are admitted into a solemn place which is not a heart at all, or even a womb, but a cranium,' says Jamie. This whole extraordinary monument was built with astronomical precision: on the winter solstice, the light of the setting sun shines the length of the tomb's entrance passageway. Visitors are rarely disappointed in Maes Howe.

The interior of Maes Howe, Orkney

It is not the quality of Neolithic workmanship that concerns us here, however. The leftovers of more recent times provide our special interest

in Maes Howe, for they give us a revealing glimpse of one of the most dramatic episodes in the peopling of the Britain Isles. At various points, more than 1,000 years ago – several millennia after the cairn had been abandoned by the ancient British people who built it – men broke into Maes Howe and covered its walls with carved graffiti. 'Ingigerth is the most beautiful of women', wrote one. 'Thorni bedded Helgi', wrote another, demonstrating, if nothing else, that the male of the species has changed little over the centuries. Another left the more cryptic thought: 'It is true what I say, that treasure was carried off in the course of three nights.' What riches these might be, no one knows.

Engraved Viking runes on a stone at Maes Howe

These ancient messages are intriguing enough. But the real excitement is the language used to express them. The Maes Howe graffiti is carved in runic letters, a form of the Roman alphabet modified – not for pen or brush – but for dagger-wielding, axe-carrying Vikings. Norsemen began using runes around AD 200 and over the centuries left thousands of inscriptions all over Scandinavia. The collection at Maes Howe is the best and most important in Britain and one of the biggest in Europe. There is a beautifully carved walrus, a serpent knot and a dragon (possibly a lion) as well as thirty sets of Norse inscriptions revealing the innermost feelings of the Vikings that made them.

But what were these people doing in Orkney? Why were there Norsemen in Britain at this time and what was their impact on our land and heritage? The long-term answers to these questions involve us in one of the most absorbing episodes in our ancestral searches, while the specific cause for Vikings' presence in Maes Howe gives us a vivid feeling for the vicissitudes of the time. It turns out that the tomb's inscriptions were carved on several different occasions by bands of Viking men sheltering from some of the mighty storms that sweep Orkney with frightening regularity.

One such incident is recorded in the *Orkneyinga Saga*, the ancient history of the Orkney people. A Viking leader, Earl Harald, and his men,

Viking longships like this one were used to raid the British Isles

were travelling from Stromness when they took shelter in Orkahaugr, the Norse name for Maes Howe, during a snowstorm. 'There two of them went insane,' the saga states. This is probably an exaggeration though conditions inside the cairn, lit by flickering, burning brands while the wind shrieked outside, must have been pretty unnerving. This was an ancient tomb, after all. On the other hand, it is comforting to note that even Vikings got spooked.

As to the Vikings' identity, they were traders and warriors who came from lands made up today by Norway, Sweden and Denmark and who began raiding Britain in the late eighth century. By the eleventh century, they had colonised swathes of land across middle and northern England as well as islands round the northern and western perimeter of Britain. They had also settled in Iceland, set up outposts in Greenland and North America, established trading stations in Russia and Constantinople, and raided Mediterranean ports, where they were known as 'heathen wizards' by the Moors.

Some scientists pinpoint climate change as the main cause of this expansion, which occurred during the Medieval Warm Period when the weather was unusually mild and stable in northern Europe. Warmer weather meant better agriculture which boosted Norse numbers. Thus population pressure drove them to find new lands. Not every historian agrees, however. They point out that Scandinavia was also going through the initial stages of state formation at the time. Petty kings had become engaged in a vicious struggle for power. 'By boosting their reputations, distributing gold and silver, foreign luxuries and weapons to their followers, these would-be dynasty builders could recruit even more retainers to their side, or eject their rivals,' says David Miles. Nor could the Vikings have got far without a number of key technological advances, in particular their longships. Made of precisely placed, overlaying planks of wood, their construction had been honed to near perfection as the Vikings established control of Norway's fjord-studded coastline and Denmark's sounds and islands.

Whatever the cause, the coastal towns of Britain and Ireland, the monasteries at Lindisfarne and Iona, and even inland townships, were exposed to the attentions of warriors bent on the acquisition of land and treasure and who were armed with the most advanced weaponry of the period. Armadas of sleek longships, manned by dozens of 'heathen wizards', swept down the British and Irish coasts and sliced into its river heartlands by sailing up rivers. Churches were razed, monks slaughtered and women taken captive. 'On June 8, the ravages of the heathen men, miserably destroyed God's church on Lindisfarne with plunder and slaughter,' the Anglo-Saxon Chronicle noted for the year AD 793. Some locals put up a fight. The great Irish chieftain Ui Neill – whose lineage we shall come across in greater detail later in this book – raised an army to fight the Vikings but was soundly beaten in battle near Drogheda. The Vikings spread, unchecked, for decades. 'The number of ships increases, the endless flood of Vikings never ceases to grow bigger,' wrote one despairing monk in the 860s. 'Everywhere Christ's peoples are the victims of massacre, burning and plunder. The Vikings overrun all that lies before them, and no one can withstand them.'

In this way, the image of the rapacious Viking invader was established and has endured in the national psyche ever since, becoming enshrined in prose and verse, from the stories of Walter Scott to the songs of Led Zeppelin. Vikings fascinate us. Indeed, of all the questions put by volunteers taking part in the People of the British Isles project, the favourite – by a long away – is the simple issue: do I have Viking blood in my veins?

We shall come to the answer to that question very shortly. First we should note one key historical point: in the end, two major Viking areas of influence were established in Britain. One was the Danelaw which stretched diagonally across the country from present day Cumbria to Middlesbrough in the north, and from Chester to London in the south. Vikings from Denmark held sway here: hence the name Danelaw, the area of England in which the law of the Danes prevailed. The second was the land conquered by Vikings from what is now Norway. They sailed west and then south, progressively establishing colonies and trading posts in Orkney, north Scotland, the Hebrides, Ireland, the Isle of Man, the coast of Ireland, and eventually the south-western tip of Wales. (As to the Vikings from what is now Sweden, they headed east, to settle in Russia

Viking invasions of Britain c.840-913

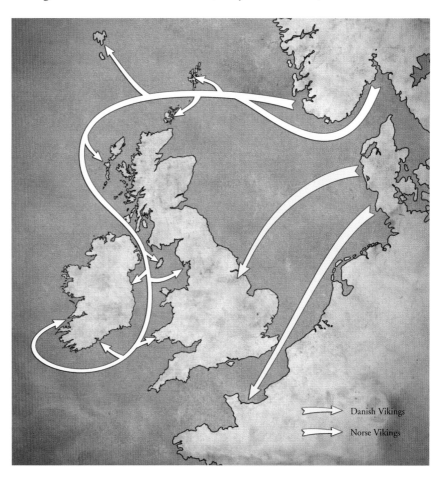

Danish Vikings

Norse Vikings

and round into the Mediterranean.) The difference between these first two Viking regions and the origin of their creators is of critical importance when trying to disentangle the biological influence of the Norse on modern Britain.

One thing is clear, however, the impact of the Vikings was profound. Consider the issue of language. Place names in Britain that end in 'by', such as Ferriby or Whitby, are Norse in origin ('by' means farmstead) and there are 850 of them across the country with particular concentrations in North Yorkshire, Lincolnshire, Derbyshire, Leicestershire, Northamptonshire and on both sides of the Solway Firth. Other names with a Viking root include those that end in 'thorp' (thorp means settlement). In addition, there is: Milford Haven, the Sandbank Fjord; Gateholm, the She-Goat Island; Fishguard, the enclosure for Catching Fish; and Lundy, Puffin Island. Further north there is Caithness or Katenes, Headland of the Cat. Vikings also set up great trading centres that are now some of the most important cities in Britain and Ireland: York and Dublin (the latter meaning 'blackpool' in Norse).

But what about people? If the Norse had such a dramatic impact on the naming of our landscape, did they also have an impact on our bloodline? Can we see similar signs of Viking influence in British men and women today? Such an observation would not only be satisfying on a personal level, it would also help in the unravelling of several key historical questions. To what extent did these Norse newcomers mix with locals? Were they like the Romans who largely kept their distance or were their interactions closer and more personal? Did Vikings take local woman as partners or did they bring Norse women with them on their travels?

The crucial question is the first one, of course and the answer to it is a gratifying 'yes'. We can see clearly the Vikings' imprint on men and women from many areas of modern Britain. Indeed, recent studies have revealed a striking picture of Norse ancestry for a large number of individuals, a phenomenon that can be most clearly illustrated in Orkney. So let us concentrate briefly on these magical islands and look in some detail at the intriguing picture painted by geneticists of tenth-century life there. Its isolated location gives Orkney a privileged status in studying the genetics of the British and the lessons learned can then be transferred elsewhere to understand Viking influence on the rest of the country.

The key to this historical detective work is the Y-chromosome. As we noted earlier, this little slice of DNA – a puny thing compared with the other chromosomes in the human genome – is passed on from father to son through generations. I have my father's Y-chromosome, just as he got his from his father, and so on into my family's past. This legacy is the biological equivalent of a watch or a clock that has been in a family for generations and which is inherited through the male line. In the case of Orkney Vikings that makes it a powerful weapon in the geneticist's arsenal, for scientists have discovered that subtle changes constantly assail the Y-chromosome. Along its twisting bands of DNA, one of its base pairs is sometimes substituted by another base pair, or one is simply lost altogether – or deleted, as geneticists put it. Over the millennia, these tiny mutations accumulate so that it becomes possible to differentiate Y-chromosomes of men from established populations in different localities, allowing researchers to tell apart the male lineages of different tribes and peoples.

In the case of the Vikings, scientists realised they could analyse DNA from parts of Britain and compare those from modern Scandinavia where it is presumed men still have the same Y-chromosomes as their Viking forebears. Men from regions of the UK who share similar Y-chromosomes with Scandinavians are likely to be of Viking ancestry. It sounds straightforward. Unfortunately, things have not proved to be quite that simple, thanks to the Anglo-Saxons. As we have already seen, these invaders from Saxony had already made a fair impact on Britain long before the Vikings arrived and had spread their Y-chromosomes through much of the population.

The trouble is that the Anglo-Saxons came from Friesland and Saxony, which is close to Denmark, and so shared a common genetic heritage with Vikings from this region, producing individuals with Y-chromosomes that were found to be confusingly similar to each other. Differentiating the male lineages of Anglo-Saxons and of Vikings from the Danish peninsula proved too complex, as Dr Jim Wilson, a geneticist based at Edinburgh University, explains. 'It is very difficult, if not impossible, to tell the difference between a Saxon and a Danish Y-chromosome at present,' he says. 'That means you cannot tell them apart in the populations of central England where the two groups fought and merged.'

But such genetic confusion does not affect Orkney. For a start, the Vikings who conquered the islands came from Norway where men have distinctively different Y-chromosomes from those in Denmark. In addition, the islands were peopled by Picts when the Vikings arrived, and their Y-chromosomes were undoubtedly very different from those found in Norsemen or Anglo-Saxons. (The Picts were descendants of the Caledonian tribes who had settled in northern Britain and for centuries they ruled the land that we have since come to call Scotland. They were skilful farmers, sailors and fishermen and spoke a version of Celtic language that was similar to Welsh and Cornish. They were therefore likely to have been similar to the ancient Britons found in other parts of the Celtic fringe.)

Orkney was ripe for a genetic investigation, in other words, and Wilson, an Orcadian and a geneticist, was perfectly placed to implement it. 'My interest in genetics grew from my experiences while growing up in Orkney, and in particular, from the Orcadian pastime of "koontan sib" or "reddan kin", the study of genealogy or family trees,' he says. 'I was very interested in this from a young age. In Orkney and in Fair Isle – where my father comes from – people know a lot about their families. And genetics is about inheritance, so it all blends in.'

These chess pieces, made of walrus ivory and whales' teeth, were found on the Isle of Lewis and are thought to be Viking

In 1999, Wilson was working as a postgraduate researcher at Oxford University and was looking for projects to establish the growing power of DNA as a tool for historical studies. Orkney seemed ideal for such work and so, having convinced his professor, David Goldstein, of the merits of such research, he went to work, taking samples of saliva from local folk which he could then compare with samples from men from Norway as well as from other parts of Europe. 'Collecting my first samples involved me having tea and scones with a lot of my parents' neighbours, friends and acquaintances,' says Wilson. 'They would say to me: "I know where my ancestors come from: they come from Norway". Others were convinced that their roots lay elsewhere, including those who thought their origins lay with the Spanish Armada which, in the case of some Westray folk, could be true. There is a community called Dons who are descended from a ship wreck on the reef at North Ronaldsay.'

What Wilson was looking for was one particular DNA mutation in which a base called guanine is missing from a particular section of Y-chromosome. This is known as the M17 deletion. It is not unique to Scandinavians. Some men from India, Pakistan and Eastern Europe carry it. However, in the British Isles, only people from Norse lands possess this mutation. Discovery of it in Orkney would mean only one thing: evidence of Viking ancestry.

Slowly, Wilson's project took its course. 'One of the first samples that I took was of my maternal uncle and he was the first for whom I saw the M17 type. I immediately knew this was unusual. In fact, it only took minutes to realise I had found genetic evidence of Viking descent within my own family. I also remember the sixth sample that I took was also an M17. Then more and more turned out the same or to carry other markers of Scandinavian ancestry. It didn't take me long to realise there is a lot of Norse blood still flowing in the veins of Orcadians today.' Subsequent analysis bore out this conclusion: the majority of Orkney men had Y-chromosomes that matched their counterparts in Norway. 'The finding was incontrovertible,' he says. It was also extremely satisfying. There, on their gel arrays and charts, researchers could clearly see evidence that Viking bloodlines had survived in some of the people of the British Isles.

This discovery was exciting enough. But questions remained.

What were the origins of those men with non-Viking DNA? Did those Y-chromosomes without M17 deletions belong to males whose ancestors had lived on Orkney before the Vikings arrived or did they belong to men who arrived after the Norse gave the islands to the Scottish monarchy in the fifteenth century? (Orkney was given as a dowry for the marriage of Princess Margaret of Denmark to James III of Scotland in 1468.) To find out, Wilson concentrated his attentions on men who possessed indigenous Orkney names, such as Flett or Linklater. These surnames are not found anywhere else in Britain. 'My middle name is Flett,' adds Wilson. 'It is my mother's maiden name and it is an ancient Orcadian name. There is a Thorkell Flett who died about 1136 and who is mentioned in the Orkneyinga Saga.' Wilson took samples from these individuals and compared their Y-chromosomes with local men, individuals who have names, like Spence, Sutherland, Sinclair or Tulloch, which are not unique to the islands and are found elsewhere on the Scottish mainland. More importantly, it is known from historical records that people with these names arrived in Orkney in relatively recent times, some time in the past five or six centuries.

Princess Margaret of Denmark

This time, the scientists discovered the concentration of Norwegian Y-chromosomes in men with established Orcadian names was even more striking compared with the general male population of the islands. By contrast, among those with more general Scottish names, there was hardly a single one with a Norse Y-chromosome to be seen. The finding speaks clearly of the establishment of a lineage of ancient Orkney families by Viking raiders whose presence on the islands has endured, unbroken, for more than a millennium. When the islands came under Scottish rule in 1468, there was an influx of Scottish culture and language. Historical evidence shows that it was only then that men bearing Scottish mainland names like Tulloch and Spence arrived, bringing Y-chromosomes of a different ancestry from those of the Norse. In other words, those non-Viking Y-chromosomes came after the Norse arrived in Orkney and suggest little male DNA on the island had been left over from Pictish times.

A Survivor's Story

Migration to Orkney from mainland Britain has occurred for centuries. Many find the islands' lifestyle, which is generally hard but independent, suits a need to avoid the crowding of mainland Britain. Hence the steady trickle of Scots, and later English people, who have made their homes there over the centuries. Not everyone has done this by the happiest of means, however, as is illustrated by the story of John Richardson, whose descendant Evelyn Glennie, the percussionist, is one of Scotland's most distinguished musicians. Richardson was a Covenanter who fought for the Scottish Presbyterian cause, which was routed at the battle of Bothwell Bridge in 1679. He was one of 1,200 prisoners marched to Edinburgh. Some were executed and some recanted the cause. The remaining 250, including Richardson, were sentenced to be transported, as slaves, to the English plantations in America. In November, they were herded into the hold of the *Crown of London* which set sail from Leith up the east coast of Scotland on a course that would have taken them round the nation's

Neil Oliver and
Evelyn Glennie

northern tip and then west to the Atlantic. On 10 December, the *Crown of London* reached Orkney and sheltered from a storm off Scarvataing, near the headland of Deerness. The winds and towering waves were too much for the puny vessel, however, and the ship was driven on to rocks after her anchor chain snapped. The captain – a man called Patterson – and his crew escaped by cutting down the ship's main mast which they then used to climb along to reach land. But the prisoners were left locked in the hold of the sinking ship. It is assumed today that Patterson did nothing to save them because he would be recompensed for those who had died on the voyage while he would get nothing for those who escaped. By any account, his treatment of his prisoners was cruel and callous. One crewman did attempt to save the prisoners, however, and broke into the hold as the ship began to break up. About fifty prisoners escaped. The rest drowned, their bodies being washed up in Deer Sound for the next few weeks. As for those who made it ashore, most were recaptured and eventually ended up enslaved in American plantations. One or two escaped, however, and were given shelter by Orcadians and one of those was John Richardson. It is believed a second man, known only by his surname Thomson, also survived.

Today, there are two families – the Rich family and the Thomsons – in Rackwick, a tiny village on Hoy in southern Orkney, that are said to be the descendants of these two Covenanters, and Evelyn Glennie is related through her mother's side to the Richs. 'I knew I had Orcadian ancestry and that I had relatives in Hoy,' she says. 'However, I had no idea about how my family came to Orkney. It was shocking to to find out about the appalling treatment of these men. I really connected with John Richardson once I heard his story.' According to Bodmer, Evelyn is 1.2 times more likely to be a Celt than an Anglo-Saxon. 'I was delighted,' she adds. 'Being a Celt and being Scottish has always been important to me and as the years roll by that sense of connection has got stronger, so it was very satisfying to have that link confirmed.'

It is a striking story, one that gives a grim vision of the tribulations visited upon so many of our ancestors. However, there is a small point in the story that is worth noting for particular comment. Consider the name of the bay at which the *Crown of London* was trying to shelter when it was struck by that storm in 1679: Scarvataing. It is scarcely a Celtic-sounding word. Indeed, it positively radiates Norse ancestry. Nor is it alone in this attribute, for just as the Vikings established a series of Norse family lineages in Orkney, they also put their names to the whole landscape. There is hardly a Pictish word left on the map of Orkney. This is a countryside peppered with places like Ysnaby, Egilsay, Inga Ness and Birsay. Thus we have a plethora of Norse surnames and place names and virtually nothing else. And to many historians that conveys only one thing: genocide. When the Vikings arrived on Orkney, they put its male population to the sword. 'The Norse invaders didn't just overwhelm or submerge the native population. They killed them,' says local historian Brian Smith.

As evidence, Smith points out that even if the Vikings had stopped just short of genocide, and instead enslaved Orkney's native Pictish population, some words and names would have survived. 'Colonisers are lazy and they are only prepared to coin a certain number of new names,' he adds. 'Yet there is only a handful of pre-Norse names on record in Orkney and Shetland: names of a few large islands like Unst. If we look at examples of other exterminations in history, we see the same picture,' says Smith. For example, on Tasmania, where white colonial settlers eradicated its native population in a very brief period, no aboriginal place names remain. The same goes for Orkney. 'There is no reason to suppose that Viking behaviour was more amiable than Viking behaviour in Iona and Lindisfarne,' he concludes.

Other historians disagree and claim to see signs of peaceful integration. For example, excavations at one Norse house have revealed a number of Pictish artefacts such as pins, pottery and combs. This find is held up as proof that Norsemen and Picts lived together. Not so, say the genocide theory supporters. The Viking invaders had simply appropriated the goods, just as they had taken the treasures of Lindisfarne, and killed their owners, just as they slaughtered the monks of Iona. This grim vision also gets support from geneticists. 'Our findings are entirely consistent with the idea of complete replacement,' says Wilson. 'I see no evidence for survival of many Pictish men. However, our work does not conclusively prove the theory. It is just possible we will one day find Orkney Y-chromosomes which bear DNA profiles that are recognisably Pictish. At the moment, there are no signs of any, however.' In other words, the Norse simply drew up on the beaches and cut down everyone they encountered, or at least every man they came across.

For his part, Bodmer and his team found strong evidence for the presence of both Viking and Celtic genes, particularly those of the islands' menfolk. 'When we analysed all the gene variants in our study, except those from the Y-chromosome, we found that the population of Orkney was about 67 per cent Celtic and about 33 per cent Norse,' says Bruce Winney, the project's administrator. 'However, when we included the Y-chromosome in our calculations, we got a division of about 45 Celt and 55 per cent Norse for the people of Orkney. In other words, the men were slewed heavily towards a Viking origin and that kind of split is consistent with a picture of the Vikings coming over and taking local women for their wives and mothers of their children.'

The idea of integration between subjugated Pict and Viking overlord is also provided from – of all places – Iceland. Vikings settled on this uninhabited island around 860 and recorded details of their arrivals in the Landnamabok, the Icelandic Book of Settlements. This tome shows that among the 400 settlers named in its pages, there were 35 who came from islands off Britain, including seven from Orkney. Could some remnants of an ancient British bloodline have been transported to the new Viking colony in Iceland? Remarkably this idea turns out to be true, according to studies carried by the Icelandic genetics company DeCode and by Oxford University researchers. Scientists already knew that Norse Y-chromosomes predominate among the island's men. The Viking ancestry of Icelandic males is well-attested. The origin of Icelandic women was less clear. So the team began analysing the island's mitochondrial DNA. As we have seen, this little

A typical Pictish engraving, found at Burghead, Morayshire

coil of genetic material is inherited through the female line, just as the Y-chromosome is passed down through the male. A total of 16,000 Icelandic women were profiled this way, and their mitochondrial DNA was compared with thousands of other women from Britain and Europe, providing scientists with another unexpected discovery: that a fairly massive influx of female genetic material from Scotland and Ireland exists among Iceland's founding mothers. More than 60 per cent had Celtic mitochondrial DNA.

'A sizeable portion of Icelandic lines of descent are tracked back 1,100 years to females whose ancestry was firmly anchored in the British Isles,' state the scientists in an analysis, published in the *American Journal of Human Genetics*. Combined with other studies, this work suggests events in the Viking era followed a rather specific agenda. First the Norse wiped out much of the native Orcadian male population and used the islands as the strategic hub for future activities in the British Isles. In effect, Orkney became a springboard for their expansion into Britain and further afield.

In AD 900, Orkney became a Norse earldom. Entire families of the nobility moved across the North Sea from Scandinavia – men, wives, kinsfolk, and retainers. It was a different matter for the warrior class, however, the foot soldiers and marines who raided and settled elsewhere. They would have been of low status, young – and single. Needing wives and concubines, they took them from female survivors of the Picts they had slaughtered. Later, these mixed families settled in Iceland.

'We found that about 80 per cent of our Y-chromosomes were Norwegian in origin and that about 65 per cent of our mitochondrial DNA was Celtic,' says Kari Stefansson, president of DeCode and one of the leading researchers involved in the project. 'It was an interesting discovery because it fits exactly with our own self-image. Icelanders think of themselves as great warriors and great poets. We would have got our fighting prowess from our Norse ancestors but perhaps we got our artistic, story-telling nature from our Celtic mothers. We were the first Scandinavians to write books, for example and to tell those great sagas. So this finding fits in very well with what we think of ourselves.'

The Vikings did not stop at Iceland, of course. They went on to settle in Greenland and Newfoundland. Both colonies died out and there is no evidence of any mixing of their bloodline with Inuit or native Americans.

However, the Norse male lineage did make it to America, but by a rather unexpected route, as we shall see later in this chapter. But first we must return to Britain, for just as we have tracked the Norse and their genes from Norway to Orkney to Iceland, so we can look at their spread elsewhere in Britain, and in particular down the western seaboard of Scotland, into the Irish sea and down into Wales and south-west England. So could Viking DNA still be detected here? To find out, Wilson's survey of Orkney was expanded to include other regions. Small towns were selected as primary targets and men who gave samples had to be able to trace their male line back two generations in the same area. Again the team found those distinctive M17 deletions and other Norse markers but with decreasing prevalence. For example, in the Western isles, 30 per cent of the men tested revealed Norse Y-chromosomes. Further south, on the Isle of Man, the figure dropped to 15 per cent and declined as the testers progressed. By the time they reached Devon and Cornwall, the evidence of Viking bloodlines disappears.

There were still a couple of surprises, however. The first was the discovery of a Cumbrian hotspot of Norse Y-chromosomes around Penrith, suggesting the Vikings set up a base there. The second was even more striking. When the researchers looked at men around Dublin – which the Vikings had established as their prime trading centre in Ireland – they found no evidence of Norse DNA. The sample size was small, however, and for many geneticists the jury remained out as far as the Vikings' impact on the Irish was concerned. Then, in 2006, the evidence was re-examined by Daniel Bradley at Trinity College, Dublin. He decided on a far broader approach to the issue and so took a series of samples from across Ireland. He then studied their Y-chromosomes for evidence of Norwegian origins. He found none. 'It was not what I expected,' says Bradley.

Undeterred, Bradley persisted in his hunt for Nordic genes. 'I decided to study families with enriched prospects of having Viking origins, in other words those which are believed to have been founded by the Norse,' Bradley says. 'Names like Higgins and Doyle are believed to have Viking origins, so it would be expected that they, if no one else, would produce Norse Y-chromosomes. So we concentrated on getting samples from men with these names and studied their Y-chromosomes. Again we got no link there.

There were no Norwegian Y-chromosomes. It was certainly surprising.'

Given the intense Viking activity in this area, an absence of Nordic Y-chromosome is certainly a puzzle. Were the Vikings forced to remain, confined, within their colony's walls, because the Irish were so hostile to their presence and prevented them from mixing and mating with locals? Or were they driven out, possibly to Cumbria, as some historians speculate? Certainly Ireland always proved a tricky prospect for the Vikings. When the Norse began raiding the country, it was already divided into warring kingdoms who were well prepared for new invaders. 'The situation in Ireland was very different from that in England and Scotland,' says Oxford historian Barry Cunliffe. 'Social instability was rife: the appearance of the Northmen merely added to it.'

Of course, the Y-chromosome is just one small part of the total human complement of genes. Our DNA gets mixed up over generations, as we have seen. Possessing a Norse Y-chromosome does not mean, on its own, that a person has a distinctive Viking make-up. The rest of their genes could have widely separate sources, depending on their ancestry. However, this is not an issue with Orkney. There was a profound influx of Norse DNA in the islands as we have seen. But does it shape local

An excavation of Viking artefacts in Dublin

people in physical ways today? This is still difficult to assess though there are clues. The prevalence of blond hair is around 18 per cent compared with 11 per cent for Scotland and 30 per cent for Norway, for example, much as one might expect from the islands' history. There also more blue-eyed people on Orkney compared with northern Britain – 40 per cent as opposed to 10 per cent. As to vulnerability to specific diseases that might have something to do with Orcadians' Viking ancestry, this is more difficult to assess. Wilson points out:

> Orkney has the highest incidence of multiple sclerosis in the world. The disease is also prevalent in Scotland and Scandinavia, indeed across northern Europe. It is therefore unclear what is going on and whether this has anything to do with Orkney's Viking past or not. Similarly there is a version of a gene called superoxide dismutase that is common in Northern Sweden and which is linked to motor neurone disease. This gene is found in 1 to 2 per cent of Orcadians, compared to 1 in 3000 of the population elsewhere in Britain. Again it is unclear what is going on. However, both conditions are now likely to become the focus of future genetic research in the islands.

Another ailment that has been linked to those of Viking ancestry is a disease called Dupuytren's contracture, a mildly debilitating deformation of the hand from which both Margaret Thatcher and Ronald Reagan suffered. 'This is common in peoples of Nordic origin but equally it is common all over northern Europe, so it is not clear if there is any link,' Wilson says.

In other parts of Britain, for instance in the Danelaw regions, Vikings doubtless left genetic clues to their presence and susceptibilities to disease but these are even more difficult to discern because of confusing background signals from similar Saxon DNA, as has been mentioned. Nevertheless, Viking and British genomes clearly merged, and the former settled down to lead conventional lives and to leave a considerable political legacy. As Miles stresses:

> The Vikings came to Britain as pirates, but in the course of the next two centuries they exerted a much more significant and positive influence. In some areas, such as Orkney, they came to dominate the

population. Their attempts to conquer England, Ireland and northern Britain stimulated fundamental political and cultural changes. They caused the break-up of great estates, stimulated a new property market and encouraged country-dwellers to move into new urban centres.

But how did this transition, from violent alien invader to political movers and shakers, take place? When did the raiding stop and the trading begin? Gradually is the obvious answer, for both activities were always considered to be parallel pastimes for Vikings, as Cunliffe has noted. 'One was never exclusive to the other,' he states, pointing to the *Orkneyinga Saga*'s depiction of the life of the Viking landowner Svein Asleifarson. 'In the spring, he had more than enough to occupy himself. Then when the job was done, he would go off plundering in the Hebrides and in Ireland on what he called his "spring trip", then back home just after midsummer where he stayed till the cornfields had been reaped and the grain was safely in. After that he would go off raiding again and never come back till the first month of winter was ended. This he used to call his "autumn trip".'

Slowly those spring and autumn 'trips' decreased in importance, it would seem, and men like Asleifarson slowly settled down to become peaceful Britons. Indeed, there is strong evidence this was always their long-term goal, as archaeologist Mark Robinson points out:

> The Vikings were responsible for a great deal of murder and kidnap but eventually used the gold they had gathered to buy land. They didn't colonise or steal estates, they bought them because they knew they were going to settle there eventually and did not want locals from whom they had stolen land to rise up against them once they had become farmers. So they tried to make everything formal and legal.

Nor should we be too influenced by gory, violent tales of early Viking raids or of those stereotypes of blond, long-haired thugs who wore horned helmets and wielded razor-sharp axes. In fact, the Vikings shaved their hair, leaving a tuft at the front, and wore conical helmets which had neither horns nor wings. Nor were they mindless criminals bent on plunder – at least not all the time. 'I think they've been unfairly treated

A Viking of the popular imagination, arriving on British soil

by history,' says Olwyn Owen, of Historic Scotland. 'The problem is that the people who wrote about them were primarily monks, and they had every reason to portray the Vikings as wicked and evil because, of course, the Vikings were pagan.' This point is backed by Jim Wilson. 'The Vikings get very bad press as their history is mostly known by the people they oppressed,' he says. 'Imagine how the history of the British Empire would read if it had been written by the indigenous populations of the countries that were colonised. It would read pretty much like the one that the average schoolboy is provided with about the Vikings.'

Yes, the Vikings went on bloody raids and yes, they had slaves – but so did most other societies of this period. The Norse also had a highly developed legal system with decisions being reached at open meetings, while women were also invested with substantial powers. They could own land, inherit and get divorced. In the end, however, the rule of the Vikings in the Danelaw area of England came to an abrupt end with the arrival of the Normans in 1066, although Norse ways persisted in Orkney for another 400 years. Nor did these political changes stop those restless Viking Y-chromosomes from moving round the globe. Having established themselves on Orkney, they were to reach other destinations, as is demonstrated in an unexpected coda to our story of the Norse in Britain, one that takes us, bizarrely, to the Cree tribes of North America.

This last part of our Viking saga begins in the seventeenth century and the launch of the Hudson's Bay Company's fur-trading empire in Canada. Stromness was the last port of call for the company's ships before they headed out into the Arctic and it was discovered that sturdy, dependable Orcadian males, reared on North Sea weather and a harsh seafaring life, were perfect candidates for manning their outposts in the Canadian

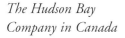

The Hudson Bay Company in Canada

wilderness. Such was their dependability and sobriety that at one time it was estimated that about 70 per cent of the Hudson's Bay Company's employees were Orcadian.

Only bachelors were hired, however, and they were required to sign up for a minimum of three years in Canada. The inevitable occurred and the men of Orkney began relationships with local women – with the secret encouragement of the Hudson's Bay Company. As Professor Sylvia Van Kirk, a historian at Toronto University, has pointed out:

> Men who had entered into kinship relationships with local women were far more likely to be trusted as trading partners. Indeed, the company encouraged a type of wedding ceremony that was referred to as 'marriage after the custom of the country'. But they didn't encourage many men to take their brides home, partly because of the reception that they might get in Britain and partly because of how the women might find adapting to life there.

When the men's contracts expired, many of these Orcadian immigrants disappeared into the Canadian hinterland with their wives to set up farms and families and so begin their own dynasties. Their impact on the Cree bloodline was profound as is revealed in the story of a treaty, signed in 1876 by seven Cree chiefs, in which the native Americans agreed to give away large parts of Saskatchewan and Alberta in exchange for reserves for their own people. One of these chiefs was native, the rest were the grandsons of Scotsmen, of whom Orcadians most probably formed the majority, and who therefore carried the M17 Y-chromosomes of their Viking ancestors. Another Norse outpost was thus created, this time in the heart of North America.

In addition, some men did bring back Cree wives to Orkney. For example, in the eighteenth century, one Orcadian, William Flett, who worked for the Hudson's Bay Company, began a relationship with a half-Cree woman. His wife left him and he returned home with two quarter-Cree children, Elizabeth and William. 'The family used to have the little Indian beds that they slept in when they first arrived, and I've given a couple of Indian embroidered purses to the museum at Stromness,' says one of their descendants, Mary Bichan, from Harray, in Orkney.

In this way, a core of people, each carrying mitochondrial DNA distinctive of the Crees, was established in Orkney, though Wilson stresses it is a small one. 'I would reckon that if you took 1,000 samples of mitochondrial DNA from Orcadians you would find only one or two with Amerindian signatures,' he says. 'It's a fascinating story, nevertheless.'

In the end, the practice of sending only bachelors was stopped when one young Orcadian woman pursued her sweetheart overseas. The Hudson's Bay Company archives tells of the story of Isobel Gunn who disguised herself as a John Fubbister and took a job with the company in 1806. At least one man penetrated her disguise, however, for just after Christmas in 1807, Alexander Henry, a trader based in Pembina, found the young Orcadian at his door. 'I told him to sit down and warm himself,' he recalls. Henry later found the 'young man' lying on his hearth. 'He stretched out his hands toward me, and in piteous tones begged to be kind to a poor, helpless, abandoned wretch, who was not of the sex I had supposed, but an unfortunate Orkney girl, pregnant, and actually in childbirth. In saying this she opened her jacket, and displayed a pair of beautiful, round, white breasts … In about an hour she was safely delivered of a fine boy.' Shortly afterwards, the Hudson's Bay Company began to encourage women to join their men in Canada.

This Viking 'colony' in the Canadian interior was a gentle incursion. Their settlement of mainland Britain had been a much more aggressive affair and had come to a conclusion many centuries earlier in a suitably violent manner. In the eleventh century, the uneasy truce between the Norse and the English broke down with the death of the English king, Edward the Confessor, in 1066. Edward had no children of his own and so he named Harold II, his brother-in-law, as his successor, a decision that went down badly, both with the Norse, who had their own claimant to the English throne, Hardrada, and with William of Normandy, who also believed the crown was his. Harold's first significant acts were therefore to defend himself and his crown from two sets of two claimants and their armies. First Hardrada, accompanied by Harold's own brother Tostig, invaded Northumbria with a vast armada of more than 100 troopships from Orkney. Harold drove northwards, gathering an army as he went, and met the Norwegians on 26 September 1066, at Stamford Bridge. Hardrada, Tostig, and most of the Norse army were cut to pieces to the extent that only 24 ships were needed to return the Norwegian army's survivors to Orkney.

However, within twenty-four hours of Harold's victory, William had set sail from Normandy with the largest invasion force to land on the shores of Britain since the Roman emperor Claudius had sent Aulus Plautius and his legions to subdue the Britons. Harold raced back to the south and on 14 October he and his exhausted troops came face to face with William's soldiers, six miles north of Hastings on the ridge known as Senlach. The outcome of England's most famous battle is well known, of course. The Normans were victorious. Harold was killed, along with the two earls who were next in line to the English throne. William, and his surviving army of about 5,000 troops, were now the masters of England.

As invasions of England go, the Norman Conquest is the one that most readily springs to mind when thinking about national takeovers. It was the last major military arrival on British soil, if nothing else. But unlike the arrivals of the Anglo-Saxons and the Vikings, it had little effect on the bloodline of the British. The Norman Conquest was more like the Roman occupation in that the country was run by a remote elite.

The Battle of Hastings, as shown on the Bayeux Tapestry

(William got so exasperated trying to learn English that he eventually gave it up and for much of his reign lived in Normandy.) Scientists cannot be absolutely certain about the lack of Norman genes in the British population, however, because of their antecedents, a point stressed by David Miles:

> The Normans, as their name implies, were Norsemen, Scandinavian raiders who had settled in Francia, married local women, descendants of the Gauls and Germanic Franks, and adopted Christianity. In AD 911, Charles the Simple, King of West Francia, granted land in the Rouen region to a warband led by Hrolf or Rollo. Over the next fifty years, thanks to fresh immigration from Scandinavia, aggression and diplomatic marriages, the Norse expanded their territory in northern France until the Duchy of the Normans stretched from the borders of Brittany to the Loire.

The Domesday Book,
1085-6

The crucial point is, of course, that Norman and Norse genes must have been similar, so it is extremely difficult to disentangle their influences on the blood of British people today. However, historical evidence strongly suggests that Norman genes are likely to be relatively rare because of the

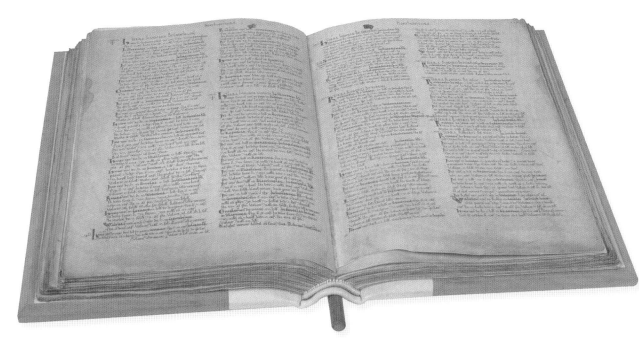

low interaction with native English people. As Miles adds: 'The Normans had little interest in the English except to exploit them.' What took place after the Battle of Hastings was essentially little more than a Norman land-grab. Nearly all the country's great estates were taken from the Anglo-Saxons and given to Norman aristocrats. French became the language of the court. English was spoken by the underclass. We still get a feel for this dichotomy today. The Normans gave us the words that became pork, mutton and beef, cuts of meat that they ate. On the other hand, pig, sheep and cow were the Anglo-Saxon expressions of the people who reared the beasts that the Normans were going to eat. The Normans' other influences on the country included the bringing over of a chunk of new vocabulary; the erection of some fearsomely effective castles, including the Tower of London; and the creation of the Domesday Book which totted up the estates of England and its workers.

However, there was one crucial move, instigated by the Normans, that was to have longlasting consequences, both for the British people, and for the efforts of scientists and historians trying to uncover more recent population movements – and that was the instigation of the use of surnames. These were introduced after the conquest to clarify the rights of ownership to land and indicate a family's place of origin. As we shall see, surnames turn out to be surprisingly helpful in uncovering past individual histories and tie individuals to locales. In the centuries that followed the Norman conquest, great population movements seized the nation through incoming waves of Huguenots, Flemish people, and others; the arrival of slaves; as well as plagues and land clearances. Combined with genetics, the study of surnames, gives us a means to follow these extraordinarily complex events and the subject forms the last main chapter of this book. But before we come to that discussion, let us stop for a diversion from the study of DNA and instead concentrate on what scientists can tell us about the appearances of our ancestors and how living in the land's different regions has sculpted their features in a myriad different ways. These reveal the true face of Britain.

CHAPTER SEVEN

Face off

*A man finds room in the few square inches of his face
for the traits of all his ancestors; for the expression of all
his history, and his wants.*

RALPH WALDO EMERSON, *CONDUCT OF LIFE*

Take a look in the mirror and examine your face. Over-familiarity with your features, and mounting disquiet about their ageing, may have discouraged self-perusal of late. Such avoidance would be a shame, however, for there is much to be learned by gazing in a looking-glass. Our eyes and mouths and ears can tell us a lot about our past. As the Hollywood actress Lauren Bacall once said: 'Your whole life shows in your face and you should be proud of that.' So take comfort in your wrinkles and pause to take a closer look at this essential piece of anatomy. If we peer close enough, we should be able to see clues not only about our ancient African roots but about our subsequent arrival and residence in the British Isles. Beneath the patina of urban sophistication – our haircuts, spectacles, make-up and the rest – we still display attributes that reveal a great deal about our past.

So let us start our self-examination with our remote past and work towards the present day. Give yourself a grin and look at your teeth. They may be pearly white or possibly a bit stained and yellowish. Either way, they should have strength, durability and – most of all – diminutive dimensions which, when you think about it, might seem a little strange. We are carnivores, after all, and virtually all other meat-eating mammals have extremely large canines for ripping up flesh. Look at your pet cat.

For a small mammal, it has fairly massive fangs. By contrast, our dentures have trouble biting through a bit of hard cheese.

It is not just our teeth that are dainty, of course. Our jaws are also minuscule. Other carnivores have large jawbones which give them enough leverage when biting and chewing. We do not. But why? What's the reason for the shrunken jaws and teeth of modern humans? The answers to these questions take us deep into our evolutionary past to a time when mankind was only just developing technology. Two million years ago, humans beings first began to construct stone tools and that had a profound impact on our appearances because tool-making, and later the use of fire, had the effect of making food – both meat and vegetable – easier to consume. We made knives to cut up meat, fires to cook it, and grinders and pounders to pulp grain and seed. The result was food that became increasingly easy to digest. Our teeth no longer had to act as heavy duty food processors and began to shrink. Our jaws contracted for

Early humans lost their body hair to keep cool while hunting after they changed from a vegetarian to a carnivorous diet

the same reasons, turning apemen with protruding muzzles into flat-faced humans.

It sounds simple. However, there have been unexpected consequences – for our teeth and jaws have not always shrunk at the same rate, as Chris Stringer, of the Natural History Museum, London, explains. 'The cues which regulate tooth growth are different from those controlling jaw development,' he says. 'The former is determined purely by our genes which are assembled at conception, while the latter responds to both genetic and environmental factors. So even in people "programmed" to have large jaws to hold large teeth, we find a reduction in the size of the former because they have been raised on white breads, pot noodles and pizzas.' In other words, people can end up with jaws that are too small to hold all their teeth because they have been raised on the takeaway wonders of modern cuisine. In early life, these individuals usually experience only a few dental problems and accommodate their first twenty-eight teeth fairly easily. Then the last four – the wisdom teeth – arrive in early adulthood. Without space to grow into, they push in at angles, erupt out of the sides of gums, or cause abscesses. The effect can be agonising and frequently requires a great deal of discomforting dentistry. Our Stone Age forebears have a lot to answer for.

As to the loss of body hair, that is easier to explain. When we evolved from vegetarian apemen into human beings, we needed to run around to catch prey and to be active. Thick hair would have allowed salt and other wastes to build up in our fur. So we lost our pelts to keep cool. All that is left are tufts on our pudenda and armpits. These lie above warm glandular areas of the body and allow hormones and other scents to linger, evaporate and disperse their intimate messages. The flight of the pheromone starts here.

Then there are our foreheads. Over the past few hundred thousand years, these have become higher and higher, the result of the relentless increase in the size of our brains which have grown as if squeezed at the front and back, producing skulls that have become taller and taller. By contrast, the human brow-ridge – the line of protective bone that protrudes over the eyes in species like the Neanderthals – has virtually disappeared and is marked only by eyebrows which may help to keep sweat out of our eyes. And finally, there are our noses which come in a

Protective Hair

The colour of our hair may be associated with various evolutionary benefits, as we noted in Chapter Two. Alternatively, it may simply be the luck of the biological draw. Whatever the reason, or colour, we have the stuff on our heads for a good reason. It protects against solar radiation. Even in Britain, summer sunshine could cause serious health problems – including skin cancer – without some cover. The explanation begs a couple of obvious questions, however. Why do some individuals lose their hair in middle age? And if hair provides such good protection, why did we lose it from the rest of our bodies? In answer to the first question, it is presumed that a gene, or a group of genes, that triggers baldness is involved. However, this does not usually manifest itself until a man has passed the age for fathering children – at least in Stone Age terms when the average lifespan was around thirty. Such an individual would therefore have passed on his bald gene, or genes, to the next generation before its deleterious effects could have had an impact on his life. Thus baldness maintains its hated hold on pates throughout the ages because it causes insufficient strain on our species for natural selection to remove it. It was a bad biological accident waiting to happen.

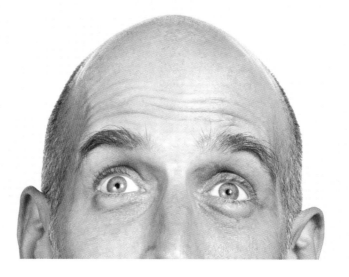

variety of shapes and sizes that are generally associated with climate: broad for people of tropical origin, narrow for those from colder zones (a narrow nasal passage will restrict the flow of freezing air into the head). In this manner, small-jawed, high fore-headed, generally hairless humans arrived on the soil of Britain and made their homes here. The question is: what happened over the next few thousand years? What can we say about the faces of the first men and women of the British Isles and how has living here changed their appearance? Such questions are extraordinarily difficult to answer. Life in Britain could have changed our physiques and facial features a great deal but without a picture of what we looked like when we arrived here in those distant days, we are stymied for answers.

All is not lost, however, for it is possible to discern some clues, thanks to scientists such as Dr Caroline Wilkinson who works in the department of Forensic Anthropology at Dundee University and who uses her knowledge of anatomy to create faces from skulls, both ancient and modern. It is a process that involves delicately replacing long-lost layers of muscle and flesh that once covered a skull with strips of clay and other materials. Given the difference between the fleshed-out faces of the living and the eyeless, expressionless visages of the dead, it might seem a business in which a great deal of licence could be employed. In fact, there is minimal room for artistic expression, Wilkinson insists. 'A person's face is determined very much by his or her skull,' she says. 'Their features are dictated by the bone underneath.' Consider the question of ear lobes. One would expect that a long-buried skull, with no flesh left on it, would give no clues to this distinctive feature. Not so, says Wilkinson:

> If you examine a skeleton's mastoid bones, the direction in which they point indicates whether a person had ear lobes or had attached ears. That is the kind of clue we use to build up faces from skulls. In addition, the bones around the nasal aperture provide an indication of the shape of the nose. Teeth tell us about the shape of the mouth while the brow and the orbital bones [around the eye sockets] let us know the shape of the eyes. Once these have been determined, the muscles of the face are added one by one to a plaster replica of the skull so that the face develops outwards. There are, however, a few details we never establish – such as eye colour, hair colour and facial hair.

An example of the power of Wilkinson's facial anthropology is provided by the case of the 'Girl from Nulde'. On 27 August 2001, the dismembered body of a young girl was found on Nulde beach in Holland. A few days later, her battered skull was found but her face had been so mutilated that it was impossible to identify her. So the Dutch police asked Wilkinson to help. Painstakingly, she worked on the skull and eventually recreated the young victim's face and head. The picture was published in Dutch newspapers and within days two family members identified the child as five-year-old Rowena Rikkers. Police later arrested her mother and her stepfather and both were jailed in 2003. As a testament to the power of facial reconstruction, it was convincing stuff.

But Wilkinson's interests are not restricted to forensic science and have also taken her deep into British prehistory. A key example is provided by skeletal remains that were uncovered during building work on a new housing estate on Whitegate Farm, in Bleadon, Somerset, in 1998. Six burial pits, arranged in an oval, were uncovered by archaeologists called in to examine the bones. One pit contained the remains of a woman who appeared to have been between thirty to forty years old when she died and who wore a brooch as a clasp for the woollen cloak in which she had been interred. In another pit, the team found a man's skeleton – including

Dr Caroline Wilkinson with Neil Oliver

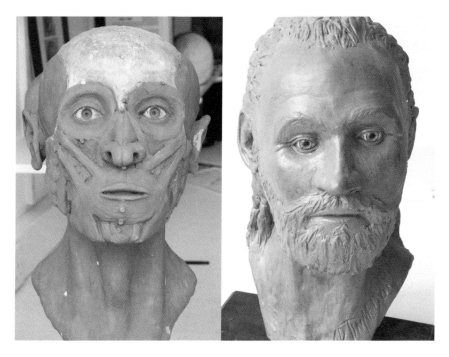

*Caroline Wilkinson's
reconstructions of
Bleadon Man*

a complete skull which was embedded in the earth. The pair were buried with large pieces of weathered limestone that had been brought to the site from a considerable distance. This was clearly a special grave. Indeed burials of any kind from this period, the Iron Age, are relatively unusual. 'Corpses were usually put on wicker beds and left outside for animals to pick away at the bones,' Andrew Young, director of the Avon Archaeological Unit in Bristol, told the *Sunday Times*.

With great care the archaeologists managed to remove the skull in one piece, only to find that when they tried to wash away its casing of soil it disintegrated into fragments. The skull then had to be painstakingly reassembled while a sliver was used for carbon dating which indicated the bones were about 2,100 years old. In addition, some mitochondrial DNA was taken from the bones and compared with forty-eight residents living in Bleadon village. (The name is said to come from the Viking era when the hills surrounding the village ran red with blood following a raid by Norsemen.) The sequence obtained from the Iron Age skeleton turned out to be identical to five of them. The villagers were confronted with the news on the BBC 2 series *Meet the Ancestors*. 'A friend jokes about us not moving far from our family roots. It shows we have a sense of belonging though,' said thirty-four-year-old David Durston, the youngest Bleadon villager to be found with a DNA match.

But if the Bleadon Man – as the skeleton was dubbed – had local DNA, did he have a West Country appearance? Could something be done to recreate his looks? It was a task ideally suited to the skills of Wilkinson – who was then working at Manchester University with Richard Neeve, another noted facial reconstruction expert. So Wilkinson went to work, carefully applying her strips of clay to replace the skull's lost facial tissue. It was a delicate task but in the end the head she produced was striking. A middle-aged man, looking slightly worried and defensive, stares at his audience. His nose is long and bent, his jaw protrudes, while his lips have a stiff, painful appearance. This latter feature, which gives the figure such unexpected vividness, was deliberate. From studies of Bleadon Man's teeth it was clear that his jawbone had to work hard grinding his food which had contained considerable amounts

Bleadon Man's skull and bones

of grit, a common feature for food produced by prehistoric farms. There were also clear signs that he suffered from painful abscesses in his gums. 'I used that discovery as grounds for a bit of artistic licence,' Wilkinson says. 'He would have suffered a great deal of pain if anything had touched his cheeks, so I concluded that he would have made no attempt to shave.' Thus Wilkinson has portrayed her Bleadon Man with a rather scruffy beard. 'As to the rest of his features,' she adds, 'his skull has quite strongly projecting nasal bones which suggests he had a large nose. He also has quite a strong brow, a big, robust skull and thin lips. His skull is fairly typical of men of the era.'

The appearance of Bleadon Man is important to our story because he came from the West Country where the nation's most ancient genes are concentrated. Thus his looks may be similar to those of the original settlers of the British Isles. More to the point, if we can establish a link between the appearance of Bleadon Man and the people now living in the West Country, in particular those of Cornwall and Devon, we would have a strong case for arguing that the first Britons are mirrored in the faces of the men and women of south-west England today. Trying to gauge what the average West Country person looks like is not so easy, however – although psychologist Tony Little of Liverpool University has worked out a neat method for attempting such a task. He creates composite pictures from digital photographs of groups of individuals. From their images, he selects common feature points – around the eyes, mouth, head and ears, for example – and from these he creates an average for each feature. Then Little builds this up to make a single composite image. The end result is slightly disconcerting because wrinkles and other facial irregularities get smoothed out in the creation of composite images, as Little acknowledges: 'The composites end up looking more attractive than the individuals who go into them.'

The crucial point is that when this technique is applied to West Country faces it produces a distinctive appearance of a person with a strong, masculine jaw, a fairly big nose and straight eyebrows. Crucially, many of these features are shared by the reconstruction of Bleadon Man created by Wilkinson. So when we look at his image, and those composite pictures of Cornwall and Devon people created by Tony Little, are we looking at features – round, distinctive jaws and big noses – that have been handed down through the millennia by the first ancient Britons? 'It is impossible to say for sure, of course, but it is quite possible,' says Wilkinson.

As to other regional variations, these are also revealed through other work by Wilkinson. She has reconstructed the head of a seventh-century man whose skeleton was found in an Anglo-Saxon burial site in Brighton. The skull – which belonged to a powerfully built, middle-aged man – has a strong cleft chin and a bifid nose, which is marked by a division into two lobes at its tip. These features are linked to a central groove visible on the bone of the chin and on the base of the nose. So Wilkinson recreated a face with a cleft chin and bifid nose as well as high cheekbones and a moustache. (Like Bleadon man, this individual had an abscess, in this case on one side of his upper jaw, which would have made shaving a very painful experience.) 'Due to his Saxon origins we estimate that he had light hair and blue eyes as well,' adds Wilkinson. The distinctive features of this man's face are a reflection of the central bifurcation of his skull. 'Bifid noses and cleft chins are characteristics associated strongly with

These are the average faces of Britain according to Tony Little, with women on the top line, and men on the bottom. They are made up from people from the following places, going from left to right: Cornwall, East Anglia, Exeter, Newcastle, Pembroke, Sussex.

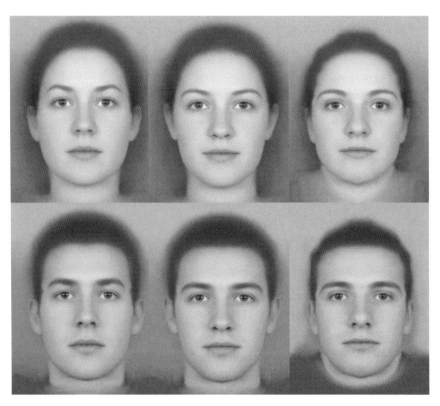

Germanic populations,' adds Wilkinson. 'They do occur in other populations but it is more common in that part of the world.'

Such a discovery suggests that a cleft chin and a bifid nose are attributes indicating origins that are Anglo-Saxon, tribes of people who were, after all, Germanic. But do we see it in individuals on the east coast of England today? The answer is a tentative yes, according to Tony Little. Just as he did for Cornish men and women, he created a composite picture of individuals from the area, in this case from Bury St Edmunds in Suffolk. 'We see the average face from this area has a slightly longer, thinner nose, a smaller jaw and more prominent cheekbones,' says Little. 'You don't see the distinctive bifid nose from the composite image. However, if you look at the individual pictures from which these composites were made you see that a lot of them do have these particular features.'

Thus between the faces of Bleadon Man and his successor from Brighton, we can see the crucial differences between the two types of people who make up the people of the British Isles: ancient Britons from

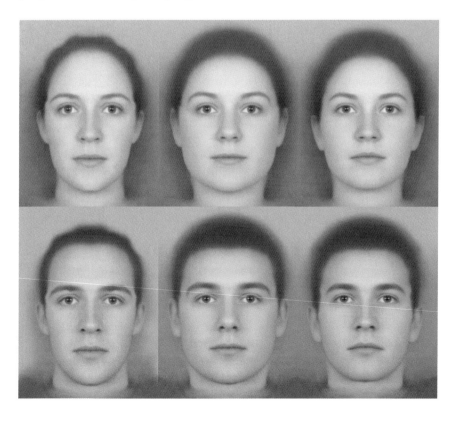

the Celtic fringe, and the men and women of the nation's Anglo-Saxon heartland. So if you want to hold a couple of images of the true faces of Britain in your head, remember images of these two faces – although Wilkinson has an intriguing alternative, as she points out. 'Heads in the days of Bleadon may have been shown to be more brachycephalic, in other words they were much wider and rounder than skulls tend to be today. And if you want to imagine a typical brachycephalic head think of Russell Crowe. His head is relatively wide and round.'

Over the millennia the variation in head shape has slowly changed, however. The general trend has been for an increased frequency in longer and narrower heads. The face of the reconstructed skull of the Anglo Saxon man from Brighton shows that this process was already well underway. This type of skull shape is called dolichocephalic and is associated with a narrower, taller face shape. 'If you want an example of the owner of a typical dolichocephalic skull think of Jeremy Irons,' says Wilkinson. 'His is nice and narrow and tall.' Thus we can see that the

Jeremy Irons and Liz Hurley both have a dolichocephalic head shape

transformation of the face of Britain has turned from being a nation of round-headed Russell Crowes into a population of elegantly headed Jeremy Irons. Or if you want female equivalents, think of a nation of Sharon Osbournes turning into a population of Liz Hurleys. It certainly gives us gives a glamorous, glossy image when thinking about the face of Britain.

THORPENESS

KINGS
NORTON
20
MILES

S
O
N
A

Chipping
Norton
10
Burford
1
Miles

A.D. 2000

MUCH HADHAM

CHAPTER EIGHT

Namesakes

A good name is better than precious ointment.
ECCLESIASTES 7:1

Fate tried to conceal him by naming him Smith.
OLIVER WENDELL HOLMES, JR.

I magine the scene. Your house has just been burgled. The front door has been kicked in and all your cupboards, drawers and shelves have been ransacked. Anything of value has been stolen. It is every householder's nightmare. But there is one small glimmer of hope. One of the burglars has caught his hand on a broken shard of glass near the front door and cut himself. Spots of blood have spilled on the floor. After running a series of DNA tests on the blood, forensic experts produce a list of half a dozen surnames of possible suspects. Police check these names in their records and discover that one, Pitts, looks promising. There is a Colin Pitts living in your neighbourhood. Armed with a search warrant, they arrive at his flat and inside find a hoard of stolen goods from several local houses – including yours. Pitts is jailed and you get your valuables back.

It is a neat story, though it sounds implausible. Getting a person's surname from their genes is an idea worthy of a science fiction novel, you might think. Nevertheless just such a scheme has been proposed by scientists following their discovery of a remarkable connection between surnames and genes in most British families. They have found that for the past few hundred years, chromosomes and surnames have been passed on in linked pairs, creating family lineages that have spread, unbroken and uncorrupted, across the country. The consequences of this web of connections is profound. For a start, it provides historians and archaeologists with a powerful new tool to unpick the movements of our ancestors. Using name-gene searches, they have already uncovered fascinating insights into some of the most sensitive aspects of British social history, issues that involve the fates of the people who were brought as slaves to this country from the sixteenth to eighteenth centuries, and in another case, on the numbers of illegitimate children that have been born in Britain over the last few hundred years. Both are vexing subjects and will be discussed later on in this chapter in the light of the data thrown up by geneticists.

Some of the most detailed work in this field has been carried out by Professor Mark Jobling, a geneticist based at Leicester University, in collaboration with his colleague Turi King. Their programme has involved the pairing of surnames with the analyses of Y-chromosomes, a procedure we encountered in Chapter Six when scientists used the combination to tease out the Viking origins of Orcadian families.

Human chromosomes

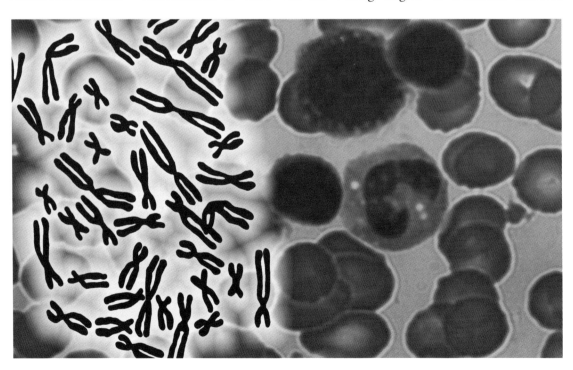

The Y-chromosome is a puny thing, containing a mere seventy-eight genes, almost all concerned with conferring the attributes of maleness. (The X-chromosome, by comparison, has a respectable 1,098 genes.) However, as we noted, this package of genetic material is important because it is handed down from father to son like a surname. They are both male attributes, after all, a Y-chromosome being, in many ways, the ultimate heirloom for a man. 'It was known you sometimes found a close connection between the two,' says Jobling. 'However our work has revealed that surnames track Y-chromosomes far more closely than previously suspected.'

There are several hundred thousand different surnames in the British Isles, about the same number of words as you will find in the complete *Oxford English Dictionary*. The 1881 census of Great Britain produced 440,000, for example. For their study, Jobling and King selected 150 that ranged from the most common, Smith, to some of the least common, including Feakin and Rivis. There are about fifty individuals with each of these two surnames compared with the 560,000 Smiths that are to be found in the British Isles today. 'We could have picked even rarer names but that would have caused problems,' adds Jobling. 'These surnames have so few people most of them tend to be related to each other – cousins or second cousins, for example. Men with these surnames are very likely to have identical Y-chromosomes, as a result. That would have distorted our statistics.' Pairs of men with the same surname were then selected from that list of 150 families – with individuals being picked at random from different parts of the country – and were tested to find out if they had the same Y-chromosome. 'We found there was a 25 per cent chance each pair would share a Y-chromosome and were therefore related to each other.' In other words, if you simply take two men with the same surname from any part of the British Isles, it turns out there is a one in four chance they will be related to the extent that they had a common ancestor in the last few hundred years.

The scientists did not stop there, however. For the next part of their project, they decided to remove the most common British surnames from their pool, including occupation-based ones like Smith and Taylor, and patronymic titles like Jones or Johnson (which both mean 'son of John') and concentrated on those with distinctive, but not necessarily rare names such as Trueman or Attenborough or Mallinson or Rosser. They then found there was now a 50 per cent chance any two men with the same surname – selected from different parts of the country – would have the same Y-chromosome. Thus in answer to the question 'What's in a name?' we get a very clear answer: it contains a great deal of information about a family's biological past.

Now the fact that the link between gene and surname is weak with common names (we shall discuss the reason in a few pages) might seem a substantial drawback if you are trying to exploit gene–name connections. What good is the link if it only works for unusual surnames, you might ask? In fact, this rarity poses few problems and for a rather unexpected reason: the vast majority of people in the British Isles have uncommon names. In other words, it is usual to have an unusual name. It sounds counter-intuitive. Nevertheless it is true. Although a name like Smith – which is shared by 1.3 per cent of the British people – is ubiquitous, there are only a few other major players in the premier league of British names: Jones (1.04 per cent), Taylor (0.6 per cent), Wilson (0.46 per cent) and one or two others. When added together, people with these highly popular names are still in a clear minority. In fact, the most popular seventy-five surnames in the British Isles represent only 20 per cent of the country's total population. By contrast, adding up all the individuals who possess uncommon surnames, leaves you with the vast majority of the British population. We may think of ourselves as a nation of Smiths and Jones. In reality, we are distinguished by our Attenboroughs, Crabtrees and Poultons.

As result, when you examine a Y-chromosome, you should have a good chance of being able to put a name to its owner. Hence Jobling's proposal that trials be set up to test the use of DNA to generate surnames. 'Our study has shown that it is possible to make a reasonable stab at a man's surname from his DNA. It won't work if their name is Smith or Jones, of course. But if that Y-chromosome comes from a Pettigrew or a Lauder or a Hooley, there is a good chance we could put a name to it.'

Jobling's idea is that a test database of 30,000 to 40,000 British surnames be set up by Britain's forensic service. Each name would be supplied with details of its corresponding Y-chromosome. Then a crime scene sample could be compared with that Y-chromosome to see if there is a match. If there is, police would be provided with a helpful lead in seeking criminals. Of course, such information would only be of use in helping to track down a suspect. Results would not be precise enough to be used as evidence in a court. Nor will the technique be accurate enough to provide police with a single name. 'It is more likely to throw up half a dozen or a dozen names,' says Jobling. 'But as these will all be relatively distinctive, fairly uncommon names, there is still a good chance you will find only one of them in your pool of suspects.' In addition, the technique would be of no use for tracing female criminals for the rather basic reason that women do not have Y-chromosomes. But given that the vast majority of crimes against property and person are carried out by men, this omission would not be seen as a major drawback. 'However, we should note that this data has only been worked out for established British names,' adds Jobling. 'We do not yet know how well this will work with new names that have come into the country in recent decades. That is why I am pressing for a trial of the system. It may prove impractical. Equally, it could provide police with a new way to home in on suspects.'

At its root, the establishment of the link between the Y-chromosome and surname takes us back to the days when the Normans ruled England. They set up manor courts so local estates and villages could be run efficiently. Part of this process involved the introduction of written records which in turn necessitated people being able to specify exactly who they were. 'Part of the trouble was that in the 13th and 14th centuries virtually every man was called John or William,' says historian David Hey, author of the study *Family Name and Family History*. 'So various ways had to be adopted to let people distinguish themselves from others.' The aim was to provide clear means for individuals to establish rights to ownership, usually of land and farms. Property was passed through the male line, so surnames followed suit. In selecting these names, some men assumed the titles of their occupations. Such names are known as metonyms. In this way, the Smiths, Fletchers (arrow makers), Taylors, Millers, Coopers (barrel makers) and Thatchers made their appearance across the nation. Every village had to have a smith, of course. That is why the name is so popular. It also explains why they have only weak genetic links to each other. Lineages of Smiths popped up all over the place, each unconnected to the next. Similarly patronyms – with which a person took a name that reflected the identity of his father, like Jones or Johnson – reared their heads across the country. Again their ubiquity throughout Britain precludes the prospect of their having any common ancestry. Thirdly, there are descriptive names, like Long or Brown and their use in different areas by different, unrelated men has also produced lineages that cannot be linked by Y-chromosome tests. (That list of different sources may sound complex but by contrast

Tracing the Attenboroughs

A classic illustration of how surnames are often linked to geographical features or towns is provided by Sir David Attenborough. The naturalist took part in Jobling and King's survey and his gene sample, along with others bearing his surname, revealed a family history of surprising compactness. 'There are several hundred Attenboroughs in the British Isles and more than 80 per cent share the same Y-chromosome,' says Jobling. 'That is a very tight correspondence and shows we are dealing, really, with only one extended family across the nation.' Nor is it difficult to trace the source of that family name, as Sir David points out. 'My family comes from the village of Attenborough which is a few miles south of the city of Nottingham. The name is Saxon. It means "at the castle" and my family got its name from the village. Generations of Attenboroughs came from that one little place. My grandfather ran a corner shop in the nearby village of Stapleford. My father Frederick grew up there, went to the local school where he did well, winning a scholarship to Cambridge where he became a don and an expert on Anglo-Saxon history.' There is also a nature reserve just outside the village, called Attenborough Nature Reserve, a home of wintering wildfowl, including ducks, geese and swans, as the Welsh and Scots have an even more confused history of using surnames. In the past in Scotland, men often took the name of their clan chief even though they were not necessarily related to him, while in Wales a surname system like today's was not fully adopted, for local reasons, until the seventeenth century.)

And then, finally, there are place names, or toponyms. These are taken from a specific local feature and form the majority of surnames today, the ones that provide us with the focus of this chapter. Toponyms turn out to

well as invertebrates such as the great diving beetle and populations of dragonflies like the four-spotted chaser and southern and migrant hawkers. 'It is a charming place,' Sir David says. 'The trouble is that most people think it is named after me. It's not. It gets its name from the village. So it would be more accurate to say that I am named after it.'

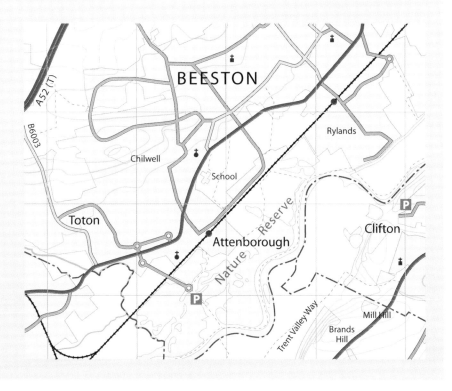

be particularly useful in historical research. For example, surnames ending in 'bottom', such as Ramsbottom, are common in the north; those containing 'thorp', such as Maplethorpe, are concentrated in the east Midlands, and 'combe', such as Widdecombe, are found most in the south-west. (It is believed 'combe' is an ancient pre-Celtic word for a valley which explains its roots in Devon and Cornwall; while 'thorp', as we mentioned in Chapter Six, is a Norse word for a settlement.)

'Essentially the imposition of surnames on the nation was an act of bureaucracy,' says Jobling. 'It was the historical equivalent of the CCTV camera and the identity card. Surnames provided central authorities with a means of keeping tabs on the population, of keeping control of it.' Put that way it sounds sinister. On the other hand, Britain is relatively new to the game compared with other nations. The Chinese imposed a system of traceable surnames on its people several thousand years ago. (By contrast, a similar scheme, to impose family names on a nation, was introduced in Mongolia only two years ago, while Japanese surnames only began to appear about 120 years ago.) One relatively late survey by Emperor Tang Taizong in AD 627 found a total of 593 different surnames, for example. This is a relatively limited number, to say the least, as Susanna Manrubia, Bernard Derrida and Damain Zanette have pointed out in the journal *American Scientist*: 'Today, about 40 per cent of the population of China have one of the 10 most common names, and 70 per cent have one of the 45 most common names,' they point out. Such figures contrast sharply with the 20 per cent of Britons who carry its 75 most common names. As to the cause of the lack of variety, the academics are clear: 'We believe that this lack of mutability is inherent to the Chinese writing system, which represents each surname by a single character.' Thus the richness of the English language has proved to be an unexpected boon to researchers in this field and has helped Britain gain unprecedented insight into its own genetic history by exploiting the highly varied naming of its people.

An early example of this combined use of genetics and names is provided by Bryan Sykes, whose study of the Cheddar Man was discussed in Chapter Three. His surname comes from a Yorkshire word for a boundary ditch and from studies of electoral registers it is clear a large number of Sykes are to be found in villages around Huddersfield. So when preparing to give a lecture on genetics and genealogy to an audience

Our placenames are often reflected in surnames

that included the then head of the pharmaceutical company Glaxo Wellcome, Sir Richard Sykes, the geneticist hit on the idea of testing and comparing their Y-chromosomes. They turned out to be identical. 'It was a wonderful discovery, one of those things that shows how exciting science can be,' says Sir Richard.

Lineages like those of the Sykes and the Attenboroughs may stretch back for twenty to twenty-five generations in some cases to around AD 1,300 and any one would have been broken by a single act of infidelity by a single woman over all those centuries. The extraordinary fact is that this does not seem to have happened in a great many families. Bryan Sykes sees this as clear evidence of the faithful nature of British women. (Infidelity by the father would have no effect on the genes of his family, of course, but if the mother had had a lover who impregnated her with a male child the link between the family Y-chromosome and the family name would have been severed for that boy and for all his male offspring.

Slavery was common until the early nineteenth century and left genetic traces in many families

Some scientists call this 'male introgression into the surname pool'.) 'We see very, very little of this in the British Isles,' says Sykes. 'These genetic studies suggest the illegitimacy rate in this country is less than 1 per cent.' That is a controversial figure, however. In the past, estimates of illegitimacy, in terms of children not conceived by their assumed fathers, has been estimated as being between 5 and 10 per cent in Britain. 'Our work flatly contradicts those figures, and indicates that family life in Britain has been a lot more stable and trusting than it has been given credit for,' says Sykes. Thus the face of Britain presented by recent genetic studies is one of striking female fidelity, it would seem. Jobling counsels caution, however. 'There are lots of complicating factors involved in studies like these – names change, that sort of thing – and we are still running our computer analyses of the name patterns we have produced, so I tend to be a little more cautious about interpreting results like these. It is clearly intriguing, nevertheless.'

There are other surprises thrown up by such studies, however, including one that also casts light on one of the key mysteries about the history of the population of the British Isles: the fate of the thousands of slaves who were brought to these shores between the sixteenth and eighteenth centuries. When Jobling and King carried out their survey, each name they used was reckoned to have a lengthy pedigree in this country, and indeed the majority threw up Y-chromosomes that were distinctively British in structure. There were a couple of notable exceptions, however. 'We got two out of our 150 who had Y-chromosomes that were not even European. In fact, when we investigated, it was clear that both were of African origin,' says Jobling. 'The important point is that by looking at other family members, it was obvious these Y-chromosomes had been present in these lineages for a long time though these family members do not have dark skin.' When slavery was stopped in the early nineteenth century, there were around 10,000 people of African origin in London alone. Dark-skinned people got rarer and rarer as the years passed but the research by Jobling and King suggests the genes of these men and women have still left a lasting impact on the bloodline of the British people. It is a fascinating insight into one of the least savoury parts of our history. 'There is no proof about how these Y-chromosomes got into these families' gene pools but it is fairly reasonable to assume they came from former slaves,' says Jobling.

The Leicester team is certainly not the only one researching the use of names and genes, however, and one group – led by one of Jobling's former colleagues, Dan Bradley, of the Smurfit Institute of Genetics, at Trinity College, Dublin, and his PhD student Laoise Moore – have produced one of the most dramatic finds in population studies of the British Isles. They took DNA samples, obtained from saliva, from a range of men across Ireland and discovered that 8 per cent of the general population possessed one particular Y-chromosome, with a cluster being pinpointed in the north-west where 23 per cent of local males possessed it. The team then calculated when the common ancestor of this pool of men would have lived and came up with the figure of 1,600 to 1,700 years ago. The date and location suggested one person: Niall of the Nine Hostages, an early fifth-century warlord who created the most powerful dynasty in ancient Ireland which was based in land now occupied by the cross-border territories around Strabane. This was known as the Ui Neill, the descendants of Neill, who ruled Ireland until the eleventh century. It is from the Ui Neill that we get the name O'Neill today. (One of the later kings of the Ui Neill was the warlord who raised the army that fought, unsuccessfully, to halt the spread of the Vikings at Drogheda, as we mentioned in Chapter Six.) The association of time and place is interesting but it is not conclusive evidence that this cluster of Y-chromosomes – which Bradley has named the Irish modal haplotype (IMH) – can be attributed to the activities of Niall of the Nine Hostages (a name that apparently reflects his predilection for taking and ransoming captives). However, further data from genealogical experts provided convincing support. Katharine Simms, an expert on medieval history at Trinity College, produced a list of surnames that have been traditionally linked to the Ui Neill. These include Neill or O'Neill, Gallagher, Connor, Cannon, Bradley, O'Reilly, Kee, McKee, Campbell, Devlin, McGovern, and O'Kane.

'We found that the frequency of this variant, this Y-chromosome, was much higher in this group,' Bradley told the *Sunday Times*. 'That was the clincher – the Ui Neill, this group that held sway and power in Ireland, seemed at some stage to have had a single patrilineal ancestor. It's another example of a linkage between profligacy and power.' In fact, the Trinity College group appear to have uncovered a population phenomenon of gob-smacking dimensions. When the team looked elsewhere at Y-chromosome libraries they found that almost 17 per cent of men in western and central Scotland carried the IMH Y-chromosome – which is also found widely in North America, with 2 per cent of men in New York estimated to be carriers. Given the levels of emigration from Ireland to the United States and to Scotland, we should not be that surprised perhaps. On the other hand, it now appears that about three million men round the world are descended from Niall of the Nine Hostages, the scientists estimate in a paper published in the *American Journal of Human Genetics* in 2006. Not surprisingly, the news of this web of relatedness was greeted with enthusiastic reports on both sides of the Atlantic. 'Listen more kindly to the New York Irishmen who assure you that the blood of early Irish kings flows in their veins,' wrote Nicholas Wade, in the *New York Times*. 'At least 2 per cent of the time, they are telling the truth,

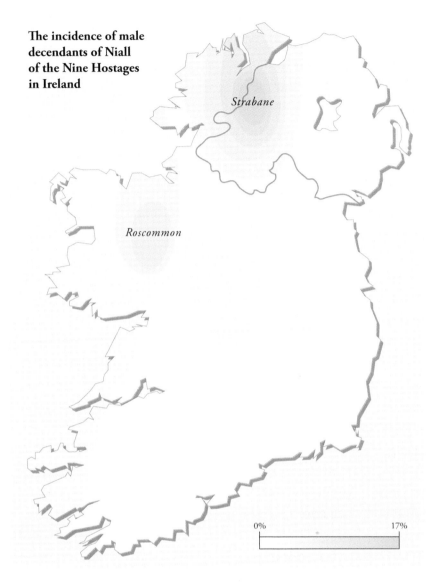

The incidence of male decendants of Niall of the Nine Hostages in Ireland

Strabane

Roscommon

0%   17%

according to a new genetic survey.'

But there was more to the study's results than providing backing for the bragging rights of Irishmen. As Simms says, some historians had always assumed that Niall of the Nine Hostages was 'merely a mythical figure, imagined in order to explain the political links that existed between the dynasties themselves in the later period'. However, the Trinity College findings 'appear to confirm that the Ui Neill really did come from a common ancestor'. Certainly, for a mythical character, he left a lot of descendants. As the scientists' paper states, Niall 'resided at the cusp of mythology and history but our results do seem to confirm the existence of a single early medieval progenitor of the most powerful and enduring Irish dynasty'. (Asked by the *New York Times*, if he had carried the Niall Y-chromosome, Bradley admitted he did, and revealed he was 'quite pleased' about the link, although tradition has it that Niall captured and enslaved Saint Patrick when he brought Christianity to Ireland.)

Providing evidence for the existence of a figure once thought to be mythical is a particularly satisfying accomplishment. The equivalent for mainland Brits would be the uncovering of a Y-chromosome cluster that links men today with King Arthur. However, the fact that the Ui Neill achieved such extraordinary levels of fecundity does raise eyebrows. Three million descendants bearing your Y-chromosome does seem rather excessive. However, there are historical explanations, according to the *New Scientist*. In its report of the Trinity College study, it pointed out that 'although medieval Ireland was Christian, divorce was allowed, people married earlier and concubinage was practised, illegitimate sons were claimed and their rights were protected by law'. One O'Neill dynasty chieftain, who died in 1423, had eighteen sons. Given these sorts of goings-on, three million descendants seems quite modest.

It is not hard to see why this combination of genetics and onomastics, the study of proper names, can be so helpful for academics trying to study past events. However, their joint use has proved to be wildly popular with the public as well, and a number of companies offering DNA testing services have sprung up in recent years. These allow individuals to gain new information about their family's origins, just from a DNA swab. Typically, for a fee of £50 to £100, you are sent a small container and you spit in it – usually first thing in the morning before you have your orange juice or coffee, beverages that contain chemicals that can interfere with DNA analysis. Then you send off your spittle. From analysis of this, details of a man's Y-chromosome can be worked out and then compared with libraries of other Y-chromosomes. This process unlocks previously unrecognised family links, while mitochondrial DNA can be used to create maternal lineages. These links are of particular value because, for dates earlier than the beginning of the eighteenth century, birth and marriage records are scarce, if not non-existent, for most families.

For example, in trying to trace my family tree I have never managed to uncover anyone who lived before my great-great-great-grandfather John McKie who lived in Ayrshire at the beginning of the nineteenth century. However, my DNA reveals that I have a distinctive Y-chromosome of Irish origins and that I am related to those O'Neill families of Northern Ireland that were mentioned in the previous paragraph. This provides me with a new way to track down my antecedents. Many other people have been steered towards fruitful new genealogical goals in this way, making this use of genetics, linked to surname studies, as much a boon to the public as it is to academia.

Of course, there is a limit to how far you can peer back into the past and make meaningful connections from the family trees you construct. As we have already stressed, the vast majority of our genes were laid down by hunter-gatherers more than 10,000 years ago. Most people in Britain are therefore bound to reveal links if we go back far enough, a point that is stressed by geneticist Steve Jones, of University College, London:

> Trace one's lineage back far enough and it will, inevitably, coalesce with all the others. Soon, they will all become branches on the universal pedigree that links everybody – William the Conqueror, Tutankhamun, Confucius, or any ancient icon who comes to mind – together into an extended family. Even a short journey upstream is almost guaranteed to unearth a magnificent ancestor. More or less everyone in the western world is descended from the Emperor Nero, rather fewer from William the Conqueror, and a mere few hundred thousand from George Washington.

Nevertheless, it is clear that the combined use of names and genetics is a powerful tool for studying the people of the British Isles, just as the two fields can make great contributions individually. We have seen in earlier chapters what the former approach, the use of DNA analysis, can achieve. So let us briefly look at the use of names, on their own, as an instrument for unravelling our past. Probably the most extensive exercise in this area has been carried out by Paul Longley and colleagues at University College, London. In 2006, they created a computer database from the most common 26,000 surnames that appeared in the 1881 census and in

Distribution of Pitts - 1881

☐ Least
☐
☐
▨
■
■ Most

Distribution of Pitts - 1998

☐ Least
☐
☐
▨
■
■ Most

the 1998 electoral register and linked the distribution of these to a map of the British Isles. The resulting website is irresistible. Simply log on at www.spatial-literacy.org. and key in a surname. You will then be presented with a colour-coded map showing its distribution across Britain in 1998. Attenborough produces a purple region of highest concentration around Nottingham; Sykes around Huddersfield; Widdicombe around Torquay and Plymouth; Ramsbottom in south Lancashire; Pettigrew around Kilmarnock; McKie in the south-west tip of Scotland; Mitchell around Dundee; Rooney has two purple patches, around Liverpool and Glasgow; Beckham is concentrated around Norwich; Crouch in Kent; and Maplethorpe in a tight grouping around Lincoln.

Indeed even the most common names show variation. Smith appears to have a distinct eastern bias, with purple pockets in East Anglia, the East Midlands and Aberdeen. Rather bafflingly, however, the town with the greatest frequency of Smiths in the British Isles is Lerwick, the capital town of the Shetland Isles. (These islands are all strongholds for the name, it appears, though Smiths are relatively rare in Orkney.) Then there are the political names. Thatcher concentrates in a corridor that stretches between Reading and Bristol, while the purple spot for Churchills is around Dorchester. As to our current party leaders, you find that, remarkably, all three – Blair, Cameron and Campbell – have roots in almost exactly the same remote part of Britain: on the west coast of the Scottish highlands. Finally, if your name is Mudd, you will find most of your kin around Darlington.

However, the real fun in using the surname database begins when you look at the map and databank for 1881 and compare them with those of 1998. Then all sorts of intriguing items of demographic information start to pop up. Consider the name Pitts, the villain behind the fictional crime that was outlined at the beginning of this chapter. In 1881, there are two hotspots for the name, Leeds and Torquay. In 1998, an extra one appears – on the Isle of Lewis. Just why a branch of the Pitts chose to head to the Outer Hebrides in the late nineteenth century or early twentieth century is a mystery. And why have their offspring flourished so well? No doubt there is an intriguing personal story involved. But, of course, that is the joy of unravelling any family history. It reveals the strange and the unexpected and the human. Indeed, virtually every surname you type into the database produces some quirk or oddity. But then every family has its secrets and strange stories, a point that Charles Dickens made in David Copperfield: 'Accidents will occur in the best-regulated families,' he observed. Hence those unaccountable outcrops of Smiths in the Shetlands and Pitts in Stornoway.

Not every name flourishes, of course. Some decline and some disappear. Occasionally a family, usually one with a rare name and few members, fails to produce descendants. The end result is extinction. On the other hand, sometimes names are simply dropped (or to be more precise, they are changed by deed poll) usually because their owners are embarrassed by them. Fartman was once a fairly popular name but appears to have disappeared for fairly understandable reasons. Similarly the use of the name Smellie has declined significantly, or to be more precise it has metamorphosed, as can be seen by a careful perusal of Longley's database. The name was once a common one around Glasgow in the nineteenth century. In 1881, the database records 1,300 Smellies but by 1998 the recorded number had dropped to 424. By any account it is a dramatic reduction, but then the Scots were always good at name dropping. Nor is it hard to see where the Smellies went. In 1881, there were 596 Smillies in the area. In 1998, there were 1,803. Thus only a little vowel movement was needed to ameliorate the affliction. By contrast, some names have mushroomed dramatically. Patel, which has its purple spots in Harrow and Wembley, has jumped from being the 24,691st most common name in Britain in 1881, to the 40th most common in 1998; Singh, concentrated around Wolverhampton, has gone from rank number 23,321 to 113; while Hussein, which has its purple spot in North London, has risen from 23,857 to 2,854. 'A very good indicator of the economic health and dynamism of an area is a good mix of family names,' adds Longley. 'It's an indicator of a can-do attitude because these days it's migrants who are making the running.'

For most names, flicking between the two maps demonstrates the inexorable spread of families from a specific heartland to other areas of the country and it is hard not to conclude that Longley and his colleagues have found a graphic way to illuminate the flexibility and mobility of British people in the twentieth century. And in a sense this is true. People over the past hundred years are now much freer to move around than in previous centuries. In those days, it required outbreaks of famine or enforced clearances to produce migrations. But to stress the appearance of new pockets in 1998 as the main feature of the database's usefulness is to miss the point, says Longley. If we compare the two sets of maps, the old and the new, the striking thing is the original pockets of surnames in 1881 maps remain exactly where they are in the maps of 1998. So yes, some people move on, but a far greater number stay put. 'What you are really seeing in the 1998 map is just a blurring of surname hotspots as a few people head off and start up lives somewhere else,' says Longley. 'In fact, the real surprise for us was the extent to which people appear to do nothing. Moving on to a new life in a new location is too traumatic for most people and so they sit where they are, getting on with their lives as their parents, grandparents and great-grandparents did before them. The idea of social mobility is a myth. Journalists and academics may move about the country but most people stay where they are.'

Some mass movements are discernible, however. For example, by analysing names around Middlesbrough, Longley and his team uncovered an intriguing spike in eight Cornish surnames – Magor, Tregonning, Trembath, Laity, Curnow, Treloar, Tremain, Olds – in the city in the 1881 census. Key these names into Longley's database and you can see the result: a purple patch for each name in Cornwall, and an intriguing orange splodge, which indicates a modest level for the name's frequency, around Teeside. This jump in numbers has been attributed by the researchers to the collapse of tin mining in Cornwall earlier in the

Botallack tin mines in Cornwall

Distribution of Tremain - 1881

☐ Least
☐
☐
▨
■
■ Most

Distribution of Tremain - 1998

☐ Least
☐
☐
▨
■
■ Most

nineteenth century. These families moved en masse to north-east England so they could take up jobs in the one industry they were accustomed to: mining. It seems a desperate, poignant act in many ways, for as we learned in Chapter Two, from the story of Ken Sweet and his mining ancestors, the occupation doomed its practitioners to an early death. Yet these men – once released from the obligation to eke a living underground – were prepared to return to mining for the fairly basic reason that the alternative would have been starvation for their families and themselves. So hundreds of them left their native Cornwall to hew the coal that was then beginning to drive the Industrial Revolution in the north-east. 'Middlesbrough was being transformed in the middle of the 19th century,' says Longley. 'In the 1830s, it was a fishing village with about four hundred residents. Then the coal and steel industries arrived. By 1841, the population was 5,709 and by 1881, it was 56,000.' And one of the key contributors to this population rise were those Cornish families who came to work in its pits. Intriguingly, you can still find all those names in high concentrations in the area.

The discovery is interesting enough. However, the database created by Longley and his colleagues contains a lot more than surnames and their geographical distribution. The researchers have also included indicators and details of economic and social status based upon their type of neighbourhood, as suggested by their postcode. Other indicators include property values, educational attainment, employment levels, financial data and health statistics. As a result, when you key in a name, you not only get its distribution across the country, you can also obtain a social ranking for it. This is expressed as 'the percentage of people with a more high status name'. For Attenborough the figure is 16 per cent. That means people who share this name have a particular aggregate social status and that 16 per cent of the British population is of a higher status than this, and are, in general, richer and better educated. For Sykes, the figure is 62 per cent; and for Widdecombe it is 6 per cent. At the very top, you find Cadbury, Goldstein and Pigden. The percentage of people with 'a more high status name' for them is zero. By contrast, when I enter the name McKie, I find that 98 per cent of the country is of a higher social ranking. (I take an optimistic view of this discovery. The McKies can only go up while the Cadburys, Goldsteins and Pigdens have nowhere to go but down.) The critical point about this information is when it was used on the descendants of the Cornish mining families, who had lived a life of grim poverty in the nineteenth century, it became clear they had fared little better in relative terms in their new home town of Middlesbrough in the twentieth century. Many of them, according to Longley, are in poor housing and some are on social benefits. Of course, the last hundred years have brought significant improvements to the quality of most British people's lives, but those families of Cornish origin remain in low socio-economic groups. It seems it may be a little harder to get out of the rut than some people think.

This trend is generally true for whole the country, Langley adds. There is far less socio-economic mobility than many people suspect. Yes, there are a fair number of individuals who rise from humble origins to become multi-millionaires or highly successful figures in politics, the arts and science. But the general picture is one of inertia. 'While some people might be surprised by the results and say it's not true of their family, the results do tend to be true in aggregate,' says Longley. 'People may have anecdotal evidence about their family doing well, but the family line can still have done badly.'

Clearly, the study of names, on its own, or combined with genetics, has much to tell us. However, it has one drawback. If focuses mainly on the analysis of Y-chromosomes to help uncover historical linkages for the

Paxman's Past

The fact that surnames are inherited on the male side can skew our perspective hopelessly. This is an unfortunate but unavoidable side-effect when dealing with names – and bits of DNA – that pass down only in this direction. It can lead to misconstructions about a person's past. Consider the example of Jeremy Paxman, one of the most adroit and combative television interviewers. He is the product of a solid, prosperous middle-class upbringing in Yorkshire that included an education at a private school and then Cambridge University. Type the name Paxman into Longley's database and you will find that only 1 per cent of the British population is of a higher ranking social order. (According to historian Andrew Phillips, the name Paxman was invented by an ambitious politician and successful businessman in East Anglia in the fourteenth century. He told authorities he wanted to be known as a man of peace and so called himself Paxman, pax being the Latin word for peace.)

It would be easy to assume from this data that the story of Paxman's recent ancestors has been one of privilege and comfort. That is certainly not the case, as the BBC's documentary series *Who Do You Think You Are?* revealed in 2006. The programme's researchers discovered that Paxman's great-grandmother on his mother's side was a Mrs Mary McKay who – after the death of her husband, John – was left to raise nine children in a 'single-end' simple reason that they track surnames so well. This bias to the male side makes it trickier to track other parts of family histories. Yet, purely from an anecdotal level, there is much to be gained from exploring other parts of a person's genealogy. And mitochondrial DNA – inherited only through the maternal line – plays a key role in investigations. The story of Jeremy Paxman's great-grandmother (below) provides a good example.

tenement in Ardenlea Street in the then grimly deprived area of Bridgeton in Glasgow. The single room had no heating or running water. Mary appealed to parish authorities for poor relief and this was granted, but only briefly. In 1901, the parish received an anonymous letter claiming that Paxman's great-grandmother had given birth to an illegitimate child. After checking local birth records, the parish authorities wrote to her to inform her of their decision to insist on 'the withdrawal of the aliment'. Mary McKay was left penniless with a total of nine children to feed and raise. The story, when revealed to Paxman on camera, produces a dramatic effect in the normally steely interviewer, who struggles hard to hold back his tears during the interview. 'She is guilty of misconduct, she has her poor relief withdrawn? She committed the great sin … of having a child,' he mutters disbelievingly.

It is hard to say what Mary's fate would have been had the Salvation Army not intervened. It was then assisting the emigration of poor people in Britain and with its help Mary sailed, with six of her children, to Canada. However, her daughter Mabel stayed behind and married one of the Salvation Army's officers, Maurice Dickson. The couple settled in Yorkshire and in 1920, Mabel gave birth to Paxman's mother, Joan. At the end of the programme, Paxman is shown a photograph of his great-grandmother in Canada, standing in a garden. 'This is someone who has been through a lot and has come through the other side,' he says. 'I am pleased about that.'

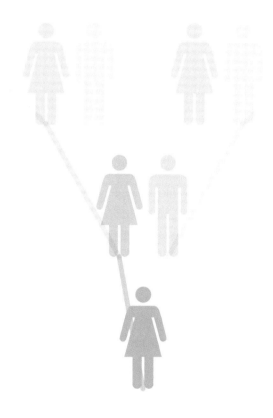

Another illustration of the use of mitochondrial DNA takes us deeper into the past and into more problematic territory. In this case, we return to the fate of one of the men encountered at the beginning of this book: Richard III, who was killed at Bosworth in 1485. Richard was buried at Greyfriars, near Leicester. Then his tomb was dug up and his body is thought to have been thrown in the River Soar. Since then, at least two sets of bones said to belong to the much vilified king have been found. Establishing if either belongs to the 'subtle, false and treacherous' Richard has proved elusive. However, a chance now exists, according to John Ashdown-Hill, at the University of Essex. After a year of tracking the king's family tree, exclusively through the maternal side, he has pinpointed a woman, now living in Canada, who he believes is a descendant of Richard's mother. The woman, says Ashdown-Hill was 'flabbergasted'. It remains to be seen if any mitochondrial DNA can be recovered from either set of bones, however, or if they match the as-yet unnamed Canadian descendant of the last of the Plantagenets. It is a promising story, nevertheless.

Thus the use of maternal lineages of DNA can also throw up equally intriguing information about the past. However, we should sound a note of caution here, using our great-grandparents as an example. We have already discussed the fact that each of us gets one eighth of our genes from each great-grandparent. (We get half our genes from each of our parents and they, of course, got half of their genes from each of their parents – which means we get a quarter of our genes from each of our grandparents, and so on, back into the past.) Thus the Y-chromosome tracks the passage of one of these one-eighth packages, the one that men get from their father's father's father. At the same time, mitochondrial DNA will track another of these routes, the one that leads to your mother's mother's mother. Your other six great-grandparents – your father's mother's father or your mother's father's mother – are ignored because we have no means to trace the zig-zag of their genetic trajectory. Yet these six great-grandparents supplied each of us with three-quarters of our genes. However, all too frequently they are ignored in genealogical research.

And think what happens when we move to our great-great-grandparents. Even more of our genetic input is ignored when we concentrate on only patrilineal and matrilineal lines. (The arithmetic works out at 14/16ths or 7/8ths of our genetic heritage which we do not trace.) Of course, at present, we cannot trace genes passed down these higgledy-piggledy routes. That does not mean we should discount their impact. Instead, we should regard Y-chromosomes and mitochondrial DNA as route-markers into our past and nothing more. If a man inherits a Y-chromosome from Niall of the Nine Hostages, that tells you nothing about him. That puny Y-chromosome carries only a handful of specialised genes, after all, pieces of DNA that have no role to play in a person's stature, character or proneness to disease, while the rest of Niall's genes will have been so diluted with the passage of time, that a descendant in New York will be unlikely to carry any of them. The same goes for mitochondrial DNA which has no role to play in the nuclear inheritance of characteristics. However, in discovering that a man has acquired an interesting Y-chromosome or a woman possesses a distinctive piece of mitochondrial DNA, we often uncover unexpected facts about our history and population movements. That is the critical lesson of this book. When we find a genetic link with an ancestor we should not think

Royal Links

On the night of 16 July 1918 – during the Russian civil war – Tsar Nicholas II, his wife, Alexandra, their daughters, and their son Alexei, were herded, with four servants, into the cellar at the Ipatiev house in Ekaterinburg, 850 miles east of Moscow, and shot by the Bolsheviks. It was a horrific, savage act. The girls were wearing special corsets into which precious stones had been hidden and these deflected some of the bullets, which were – in any case – fired by gunmen of dubious competency. Several victims had to be clubbed and stabbed to death, it was later alleged. Sulphuric acid was poured over the corpses and they were buried in a shallow grave. The fate of the Romanovs shocked Europe and continued to fascinate the world.

With the collapse of the Soviet Union in the 1990s, historians started to look for the Romanovs' burial pit, and eventually discovered the skeletons. The only problem was the issue of proving the bones were those of the Russian royal family: all their flesh and tissue had been destroyed. However, there was one possible technique that could be used, scientists realised. There was a chance some mitochondrial DNA could be found in traces in their bone cells. The prospect was encouraging enough to bring Dr Pavel Ivanov, a leading Russian forensic scientist, to Britain with bits of Romanov bones in the boot of his hired car. Experts, led by Dr Peter Gill, at the Forensic Science Service at Aldermaston, extracted tiny samples of mitochondrial DNA from the bones and with each one, produced a sequence. The question it provides evidence of an inherited predisposition (the MC1R gene and red hair, being an exception) and instead view it only as a marker that reveals aspects of our history that might never have been established by other means.

Such uses of genetics have provided us with powerful way of looking at the past, as the preceding pages have shown. That is the story of the face of Britain. However, before we leave our investigation, we need to address one final issue: where do we go from here?

was: with whom could they compare these sequences to prove they belonged to the Romanovs? The answer was provided by our own royal family. The grandmother of Prince Philip was the tsarina's sister. Both Prince Philip and Tsarina Alexandra therefore possessed the same mitochondrial DNA. So a blood sample was taken from the prince. His sequence matched not only those of Tsarina Alexandra, but those found in all of the bones from children discovered in the burial pit. At the same time, DNA taken from two unnamed relatives of the tsar was found to match DNA taken from the skeleton presumed to belong to Nicholas II. The Russian authorities were convinced and had all the skeletons reburied at a special ceremony in St Petersburg, the country's old imperial capital in 1998.

EPILOGUE

The Lost World

We ignore the intimate relatedness of all humans
when we look for and amplify the minutest distinctions
among us, until we find ourselves surrounded by what
look more like our natural enemies than members of
our own close-knit species.

ERIC HARTH, *DAWN OF THE MILLENNIUM*

If there has been a common theme to the words of the men and women who have given blood to the People of the British Isles project, it is one that focuses on the prospect of imminent loss. The situation is best summed up by Ken Sweet, who we encountered in Chapter Two and whose family has lived around St Austell in Cornwall for hundreds of years. His children have moved away from the area and his grandchildren are unlikely to return, he says. 'When they go, the thread that has linked my family for centuries to this land will have been broken.' It is a sobering prospect. Yet it is one shared by nearly all the participants of this great undertaking. Most speak of the likelihood of their family's connection with their birthplace being cut in the near future, a grim situation – though this imminent break-up also shows how timely has been the setting up of Bodmer's venture. The country is likely to have good reason to thank the geneticist when the project is completed in 2009, for its results are destined to reveal a staggering amount about the British Isles and its people. At the same time, it is unlikely that such a programme will ever be repeated. This is our one real chance to use genetics to peer into the mists of our prehistory and study, in detail, how its population was created and established. The opportunity will not be repeated because rural life, a fixed feature of the British Isles for millennia, is changing with unsettling rapidity.

It is therefore worth emphasising what has already been achieved and to stress the significance of the results already produced by Bodmer and his team, and by other scientists working on similar programmes. In the case of the People of the British Isles project, its researchers have uncovered evidence that links men and women today to the handful of settlers who first came to this land when it was still attached to the continent. It has been one of the thrills of this project to see signs of the genes of these ancient folk in the gels and arrays in the team's Oxford laboratory. The first people to establish the bloodline of the British and Irish, we should remember, were made up of only a few hundred, possibly a couple of thousand, hunter-gatherers who settled in here more than 12,000 years ago. Yet we can see clear signals today of their presence in our genes. Science rarely gets much closer or more personal than this. In fact, it now appears that around half our gene pool is based on the DNA that we have inherited from our Stone Age ancestors.

At the same time, we can also see – in the blood of many of the families of middle England – the tell-tale genetic signature of the Anglo-Saxons, that other great biological influence on the nation. They too have contributed up to 50 per cent of the genes in some parts of the British Isles. Thus the Anglo-Saxons not only gave us the language that we speak today but a large chunk of our biological heritage. In addition, there are those samples taken from people from outlying parts of the British archipelago that reveal the influence of those romantic, feared individuals, the Vikings, another group that has played a key role in establishing lineages in this country. We can even detect the more subtle influences that some of these different people have had on the faces of the nation. In total, this work represents a remarkable achievement for science and for our understanding of ourselves.

However, we should note that this undertaking is not yet complete. Indeed it is one of the key concerns of Bodmer and his colleagues that more volunteers should come forward to give blood and to maintain the momentum of their initial successes. Thousands of individuals – men and women who can show that their ancestry in Britain's rural corners goes back three or more generations – are needed to give blood to keep up the momentum of the People of the British Isles project. This, then, is the way forward – for individuals who fit the project's strict protocols to give blood. This is their last chance, and ours, to learn about our remarkable biological past.

Appendix

Deoxyribonucleic Acid, or DNA. Discovered by the Swiss chemist Johann Meischer in the late nineteenth century, DNA was only conclusively shown to be the carrier of genetic information in the human body when James Watson and Francis Crick carried out their classic studies in the 1950s. The pair, based at Cambridge's Cavendish Laboratory, showed that the molecule was made up of a long, twisting staircase of chemicals, a double helix. The long filaments that make up the banisters of this microscopic staircase consist of chemicals known as bases, and which are generally remembered by their initial letters: adenine (A); cytosine (C); guanine (G) and thymine (T).

When a cell divides, so does its DNA. Its double helical strands of A, C, G and T bases separate and each grows a new second chain, with the result that an exact copy of the originator's genetic script is created. The new helix then migrates to a new cell and directs the manufacture of proteins. A mere six million millionths of a gram of DNA is created each time a cell divides, yet it carries as much information as ten volumes of the *Oxford English Dictionary*. Small wonder that Watson described the DNA molecule, whose structure he had exposed, as 'the Rosetta stone that unravels the true secret of life'. For his part Crick wrote to his son Michael to tell him 'we think we have found the basic mechanism by which life comes from life'. Both were right, of course.

We should note, however, that there are two types of DNA within our bodies. There is mitochondrial DNA and there is nuclear DNA. The latter makes up the genes which control the development of the growing body and which determines if we are going to have red hair or blue eyes. This type of DNA is found in the nucleus of every cell in our body and is bundled together into chromosomes, along which are ranged those genes for red hair and blue eyes. We each have 23 pairs of chromosomes numbered from one to 22, plus either a couple of X-chromosomes, or a Y and an X. The former combination dictates that a person will be a woman, while the presence of a Y-chromosome ensures the masculinity of its owner.

And then there is mitochondrial DNA. This is found outside the nucleus, but inside the cell, in objects called mitochondrial organelles which act as the power packs for our cells. Mitochondrial DNA differs from nuclear DNA in one important manner. Nuclear DNA is bequeathed to us as a 50–50 mix from both our parents. Mitochondrial DNA is passed on to us only from our mothers. We should also note that there is a direct corollary to this pattern of inheritance for men. The Y-chromosome too is inherited only by one sex, this time males, and so a man is passed his Y-chromosome from his father, who got that from his father and so on into the mists of time.

Polymerase Chain Reaction, or PCR. Perhaps the most important invention for exploiting DNA as a tool for historical research is that of DNA amplification. Also known as polymerase chain reaction, or PCR, this technique was invented by Kary Mullis, and developed by scientists led by Henry Erhlich, of the Cetus Corporation, in California, in the 1980s. Its impact has been profound as the normally restrained journal *Nature* once acknowledged, describing the technique as one that has 'revolutionised molecular biology'. For a description of PCR, we need look no further than the words of Kary Mullis himself. 'Beginning with a single molecule of the genetic material DNA, the PCR can generate 100 billion similar molecules in an afternoon,' he says. 'The reaction is easy to execute: it requires no more than a test tube, a few simple reagents and a source of heat. The DNA sample that one wishes to copy can be pure, or it can be a minute part of an extremely complex mixture of biological materials. The DNA may come from a hospital tissue specimen, from a single human hair, from a drop of dried blood at the scene of a crime, from the tissues of a mummified brain or from a 40,000-year-old woolly mammoth frozen in a glacier.' Short of a magic wand, a molecular biologist could scarcely ask for anything more powerful.

What Mullis realised – during a midnight drive from San Francisco to his cabin in nearby Mendocino County – was that he could exploit the way that DNA splits apart inside a cell as it divides and grows. Normally this process involves the two strands of the double helix pulling apart and each growing a new complimentary strand to produce two double helices. But if he carefully controlled conditions in the laboratory, providing all the right nutrients and chemical reagents found in cells, Mullis realised he could stop and then restart his reaction, by raising and lowering temperatures at crucial times, in such a way that he would make not just two copies of a piece of DNA but he could double his numbers of these sections every twenty minutes or so. Essentially he realised he could create a chain reaction and the chemical he used to drive it was an enzyme called polymerase. In the cells of our bodies, this is responsible for stitching together the building blocks of genes into full-length strands of DNA. Hence the subsequent naming of Mullis's brainchild: polymerase chain reaction. As a title, it is highly accurate, of course, but it completely fails to convey the incredible power of the technique, a point that Mullis realised from the moment he conceived of his grand idea.

'Excited, I started running powers of two in my head: 2, 4, 8, 16, 32 … I remembered vaguely that two to the tenth power was about 1,000 and that therefore two to the twentieth power was around 1,000,000. I stopped the car at a turnout overlooking Anderson Valley. From the glove compartment I pulled a pencil and paper – I needed to check my calculations. Jennifer, my sleepy passenger, objected groggily to the delay and the light but I exclaimed that I had discovered something fantastic. Unimpressed, she went to sleep.' Not since James Watt wandered across Glasgow Green and dreamed up the idea of the secondary condenser for the steam engine, an inspiration that set loose the Industrial Revolution, has a single, momentous idea been so well recorded in time and place. Given its impact, and the ingenuity of the technique, it was scarcely surprising that Mullis received a share of the 1993 Nobel Prize for Chemistry for his achievement in inventing PCR.

Of course, when scientists use PCR, they don't grow billions of copies of entire double helices. They only seek out a small section that is of particular interest to them. This is done using chemicals called oligonucleotides which sit at either end of the desired piece of DNA so that only the section in between is grown up. Then a billion copies of this piece of DNA can be made, enough for researchers to carry out all their tests and studies with consummate ease. This technology, with refinements, has been crucial in unravelling our genetic history, as archaeologist Professor Martin Jones, of Cambridge University, has put it.

'PCR is now a key molecular tool that has transformed all aspects of DNA research, not least the quest for ancient DNA.'
Source: *The Book of Man: The Quest to Discover Our Genetic Heritage*, Walter Bodmer and Robin McKie (Little, Brown).

Radiocarbon dating. No technology has had a greater impact on the unravelling of our past than this ingenious invention. Radiocarbon dating exploits one of the key physical processes that affect our planet. Streams of particles from outer space constantly bombard the upper atmosphere, creating a cascade of other particles. Some of these secondary particles strike atoms in the atmosphere. One key reaction occurs when a particle called a neutron hits an atom of nitrogen. When this happens, a different element, carbon, is created although this carbon atom is of a special type, known as carbon-14. Unlike the other atoms of carbon on Earth, carbon-14 is slightly radioactive and slowly decays over time and at a uniform rate. For any piece of carbon-14, after about 5,700 years, half its weight is left; after about 11,400 years a quarter; and after about 17,000 years, an eighth. From this constant halving, we get the term half-life. For carbon-14 that 'half-life' is 5,700 years.

Now, the Earth's supply of carbon-14 would have run out long ago at that this rate of decay were it not for the constant supply of new atoms appearing at the top of our atmosphere. These atoms sink towards Earth, mix with oxygen atoms as they descend, form carbon dioxide and are eventually absorbed by plants and trees. Some of this plant material is eaten by animals. Thus, by measuring how much radiocarbon a piece of plant, charcoal or bone contains, a reasonable estimate of its age can be obtained. Essentially, all you do is measure its radioactivity.

The technique is of immense power (though it has limitations as we shall see) and rightly earned its inventor, the chemist Willard Libby, from Chicago University, a Nobel Prize, in 1960. Radiocarbon dating was first used to produce dates for several ancient Egyptian sites. These fitted well with previous estimates and the technology quickly earned respectability. Then came the surprises. Thanks to radiocarbon dating it was found that Stonehenge must have been built a thousand years earlier than previously believed, while the birth of farming in the Middle East was shown to be about 10,000 years old, double some previous estimates.

However, radiocarbon dating's greatest impact on public imagination came when it was used to solve a fossil riddle that had captivated Britain for several decades: the mystery of the Piltdown skull. Found in 1912, in a gravel pit in Sussex, not far from Boxgrove, the skull had an apelike jaw and a large, modern-looking braincase. British scientists – desperate for finds as remarkable as those that had been made in the nineteenth century at Cro-Magnon in France and in the Neander valley in Germany – pounced on the discovery and hailed it as the 'missing link' between humans and apes. But as the years passed, and subsequent discoveries of apemen were made, the Piltdown skull proved to be quite unlike anything found elsewhere. Suspicions mounted until, in 1953, stringent tests showed the skull was probably a fake, an amalgam of a human braincase and an orang-utan jaw, chemically stained to give it an ancient appearance. So archaeologists turned to the fledgling science of radiocarbon dating – which revealed the bones were only a few hundred years old. The Piltdown skull was a fraud. To this day, its perpetrator remains unidentified.

There are restrictions to the effectiveness of radiocarbon dating, however. Those diminishing fractions of samples reach a limit. After about 35,000 years, less than 2 per cent of a sample's original radiocarbon will remain. These dangers posed to accurate measurement are stressed by Chris Stringer of the Natural History Museum, London. 'Material could have been poorly preserved, so that its carbon will have been lost, if, for example, it was buried in acidic soil,' he says. 'Even worse, any slight contamination with carbon from another source has a severe effect. When dating a very old sample it would appear to be 4,000 years younger than it really is if an impurity of only one per cent of new carbon was added to it.'

Such dangers mean that scientists now treat dates, produced by this technology, of more than 30,000 years with considerable caution. This has problems when dealing with finds of deep antiquity. However, for the history of the occupation of the British Isles by *Homo sapiens*, radiocarbon dating has done very nicely indeed.

Source: *African Exodus: The Origins of Modern Humanity*, Chris Stringer and Robin McKie (Jonathan Cape).

Acknowledgements

A great many scientists, archaeologists and historians contributed valuable time in helping me write *The Face of Britain*. Without their generosity, it would have been an impossible task. I am immensely grateful to them as a result. Indeed, it has been a real pleasure to be involved in such an intriguing subject with the assistance of so many distinguished, enthusiastic experts. In particular, I am indebted to David Miles, the chief archaeological adviser to English Heritage for his advice, time and patience and also for his encouragement and good cheer and for his suggestions for improving chapter drafts.

I would also like to record my gratitude to Chris Stringer, of the Natural History Museum, London, with whom I have collaborated on several previous projects, including our book *African Exodus*. Chris was also a key source of information for my own book *Apeman* (BBC), and once more he has provided patient guidance during my writing of *The Face of Britain*. His own book, *Homo britannicus*, published by Penguin in 2006 gives a superb insight into the early days of the human occupation of the British Isles.

I am also very grateful to Walter Bodmer for his encouragement and help in writing this book. His achievement in establishing the People of the British Isles project is destined to transform the study of the history of Britain. I would also like to extend my thanks to the project's manager, Bruce Winney, for his patience, help and good cheer.

Among the other scientists and historians who were of such help were Steven Aldhouse-Green, Paul Bahn, Larry Barnham, Clive Gamble, Ian Jackson, Mark Jobling, Paul Longley, Jonathan Rees, Lord Colin Renfrew, Martin Richards, Charlotte Roberts, Mark Robinson, Ian Shennan, Kari Stefansson, Dallas Swallow, Mark Thomas, Caroline Wilkinson, and Jim Wilson.

I would also like to thank Nick Godwin and his colleagues at WagTV for their companionship and help. In addition, I should record my debt to Roger Alton, Paul Webster, Kamal Ahmed and Lucy Rock at the

Observer for their support, as well as the staff of the research department of the *Guardian* and *Observer* newspapers for their assistance in gathering material for the book. As usual, my agent Caradoc King, at AP Watt – with his colleagues Elinor Cooper and Judith Evans – was tireless in his efforts to assist me.

Most of all though, I am indebted to my wife Sarah who not only read my chapters and spotted each one's errors and inconsistencies but who also tolerated, with considerable patience, the monster who lurked in our attic study during the writing of this book.

Sources and further reading

A key source used in the writing of *The Face of Britain* was David Miles's superb account of the peopling of our islands, *The Tribes of Britain,* published by Weidenfeld & Nicolson. The book gives a magnificent overview of the historical processes that have shaped our population and is supported by the detailed archaeological knowledge of the author, who is chief archaeological adviser to English Heritage. David not only demonstrates a commendable light touch in his writing but possesses an immensely impressive knowledge about his subject. For anyone seeking to take this fascinating subject further, *The Tribes of Britain* can be strongly recommended.

I also found Francis Pryor's *Britain BC: Life in Britain and Ireland before the Romans,* and its companion volume, *Britain AD: A Quest for Arthur, England and the Anglo-Saxons,* both published by Harper Perennial, to be highly enjoyable, stimulating reads. Again the perspective is authoritative and the style highly readable.

Other fine books on the subject include Barry Cunliffe's *Facing the Ocean: The Atlantic and its People*, Oxford University Press, and Simon Schama's *History of Britain: 3000 BC to AD 1603*, BBC; Melyvn Bragg's *The Adventure of English*, Sceptre; and Jeremy Paxman's *The English*, Penguin. A final treat was to discover that *1066 And All That*, by W.C. Sellar and R.J. Yeatman, Penguin, is still as achingly funny as I found it in my youth.

In addition, to the books mentioned above, the following were also consulted in the writing of the following individual chapters.

Chapter One: Blood Count
The Book of Man, Walter Bodmer and Robin McKie, Abacus
The Kingdom by the Sea, Paul Theroux, Penguin
Self-Made Man and his Undoing, Jonathan Kingdon, Simon & Schuster

Chapter Two: Red Shift
African Exodus: The Origins of Modern Humanity, Chris Stringer and Robin
  McKie, Jonathan Cape

The Invention of Tradition, edited by Eric Hobsbawm and Terence Ranger, Cambridge University Press

Archaeology & Language: The Puzzle of Indo-European Origins, Colin Renfrew, Pimlico

Chapter Three: Home Alone

Paviland Cave and the 'Red Lady', Stephen Aldhouse-Green, Western Academic & Specialist Press, Bristol

Apeman, Robin McKie, BBC

Fairweather Eden, Michael Pitts and Mark Roberts, Century

African Exodus: The Origins of Modern Humanity, Chris Stringer & Robin McKie, Jonathan Cape

The Seven Daughters of Eve, Bryan Sykes, Bantam Press

The Human Odyssey: Four Million Years of Human Evolution, Ian Tattersall, Pentrice Hall

Chapter Four: From Hazelnuts to Henges

The Rise and Fall of the Third Chimpanzee, Jared Diamond, Radius

The Molecule Hunt, Martin Jones, Penguin

After the Ice: A global history 20,000-5,000 BC, Steven Mithen, Weidenfeld & Nicolson

Chapter Five: Word Power

The English: A portrait of a people, Jeremy Paxman, Penguin

The Adventure of English: The Biography of Language, Melvyn Bragg, Sceptre

1066 and All That. W.C. Sellar and R.J. Yeatman, Penguin.

Britain AD: A quest for Arthur, England, and the Anglo-Saxons, Francis Pryor, Harper Perennial

Chapter Six: Hammer of the Gods

Facing the Ocean, The Atlantic and its Peoples, Barry Cunliffe, Oxford University Press

The Little Ice Age, Brian Fagan, Basic Books

Findings, Kathleen Jamie, Sort of Books

The Blood of the Vikings, Julian Richards, Hodder & Stoughton

Chapter Eight: Namcsakcs

The Adventure of English, Melyvn Bragg, Sceptre

The English, Jeremy Paxman, Penguin

In The Blood: God, Genes and Destiny, Steve Jones, Harper Collins

Apart from the books mentioned above, a range of scientific papers and other written sources were consulted in the writing of this book. These include:

Chapter One: Blood Count

The Greatest Journey, James Shreeve, National Geographic, pp61-73, March 2006

Chapter Two: Red Shift

Pleiotropic effects in melanocortin 1 receptor (MC1R) gene on human pigmentation, Jonathan Rees, Human Molecular Genetics, 2000, vol 9, No17 2531-2537

Celt Appeal, Tom O'Neill, National Geographic, pp74-95, March 2006

Chapter Three: Home Alone

Paviland Cave: contextualising the 'Red Lady', Stephen Aldhouse-Green & Paul Pettit, Antiquity 72 (1988): 756-72

The Archaeological and Genetic Foundations of the European Populations during the Late Glacial, Clive Gamble et al, Cambridge Archaeological Journal, 15:2, 193-223, 2005

Odd Man Out: Neanderthals and Modern Humanity, Paul Pettitt, British Archaeology, February, 2001, pp. 8-13

The Neolithic Invasion of Europe, Martin Richards, Annual Review of Anthropology, 2003, 32:135-62

The Population of Later Upper Palaeolithic and Mesolithic Britain, Christopher Smith, Proceedings of the Prehistoric Society, volume 58, 1992, pp 37-40

Chapter Four: From Hazelnuts to Henges

Swallow, D. M. and Hollox, EJ. (2000) *The genetic polymorphism of intestinal lactase activity in adult humans*. Chapter 76 in "Metabolic basis of inherited disease" 8th edition eds Scriver, C. R., Beaudet, A. L. Sly, W. S. Valle, D. McGraw-Hill Vol 1 , pp 1651-1663.

Chapter Five: Word Power

Y Chromosome Evidence for Anglo-Saxon Mass Migration, M. Weale et al, Molecular Biology and Evolution, 19 (7): 1008-1021, 2002

A Y-Chromosome Census of the British Isles, David Goldstein et al, Current Biology, Vol 13, 979-84, May 27, 2003

Chapter Six: Hammer of the Gods

Genetic evidence for different male and female roles during cultural transitions in the British Isles, James Wilson et al, Proceeding of the National Academy of Science, volume 98, number 9, 5078-83

Estimating Scandinavian and Gaelic Ancestry in the Male Settlers of Iceland, Agnar Helgason et al, American Journal of Human Genetics, Vol 67, 697-717, 2000

MtDNA and the Origin of the Icelanders: Deciphering Signals of Recent Population History, Agnar Helgason et al, American Journal of Human Genetics, Vol 66

MtDNA and the Islands of the North Atlantic: Estimating the Proportions of Norse and Gaelic Ancestry, Agnar Helgason et al, American Journal of Human Genetics. Vol 68, 2001

Chapter Eight: Namesakes

The quantitative analysis of family names: historic migration and the present day neighbourhood structure of Middlesbrough, United Kingdom, P A Longley, R Webber, D Lloyd, Annals of the Association of American Geographers 96: 1040-59 in press

Focus: Jeremy Paxman fought back tears when he discovered that his ancestor was forced to live in squalor, Kenny Farquharson, Sunday Times, 11 December, 2005

High King Niall: the most fertile man in Ireland, Jan Battles, Sunday Times, 15 January, 2006

If the Irish Claim Nobility, Science May Approve, Nicholas Wade, The New York Times, January 18, 2006

Medieval Irish warlord boast three million descendants, New Scientist, 18 January, 2006

Genealogy in the Age of Genomics, Susanna Manrubia, Bernard Derrida, and Damian Zanette, American Scientist, March-April 2003, Volume 91, pp 158-165

PICTURE CREDITS

Timeline

Neandertal man *Homo neanderthalensis*: artist D. Maurice Wilson/Natural
History Museum

Hadrian's Wall: Getty Images

Homo heidelbergensis: Natural History Museum

Red deer axes: Natural History Museum

Pottery bowl: British Museum

Penny of Offa, King of Mercia, 757-96: © Fitzwilliam Museum, University
of Cambridge, UK/Bridgeman Art Library

Henry VII: National Portrait Gallery

The Beatles: Redferns/Music Pictures

Bayeux Tapestry: Bridgeman Art Library

Lewis chessmen: British Museum

William Shakespeare: Corbis

Chapter One

Henry VII: National Portrait Gallery

Penny of Offa, King of Mercia, 757-96: © Fitzwilliam Museum, University of
Cambridge, UK/Bridgeman Art Library

Cerne Abbas Giant: Alamy

Strands of DNA: Getty Images

Francis Crick and James Watson: A. Barrington Brown/Science Photo Library

Neandertal family *Homo neanderthalensis*: Maurice Wilson/Natural History
Museum

Chapter Two

'Lady Lilith', 1868 Dante Charles Gabriel Rossetti, (1828-82) © Delaware Art
Museum, Wilmington, USA/Bridgeman Art Library

Cornish tin miners at Redruth Mine, circa 1923: Topical Press Agency/Getty
Images

Boudicca, Queen of the Iceni: illustration by A S Forrest in *Our Island Story* by
H E Marshall. Mary Evans Picture Library/Edwin Wallace

Prince Harry: Pool/Tim Graham Picture Library/Getty Images

Oliver Cromwell: National Portrait Gallery

Patsy Palmer: Camera Press/James Veysey

Catherine Tate: © Rune Hellestad/Corbis

Queen Elizabeth I: National Portrait Gallery

Greg Rutherford: Reuters/Ruben Sprich

Nell Gwyn (1650-87) by Sir Peter Lely (1618-80): Sudbury Hall, Derbyshire, UK/Bridgeman Art Library

Stone ornament detail on a celtic cross Ireland © Philipp Mohr/Alamy

Chapter Three

Homo heidelbergensis, Boxgrove Man by John Sibbick: Natural History Museum

Boxgrove excavation site: Natural History Museum

The killing floor of *Homo heidelbergensis*, Boxgrove Man by John Sibbick: Natural History Museum

Homo heidelbergensis, Boxgrove Man tibia: Natural History Museum

Model head of Neandertal man (*Homo neanderthalensis*) by Maurice Wilson: Natural History Museum

Model head of *Homo sapiens*, Cro-Magnon man by Maurice Wilson: Natural History Museum

Caribou herd migrating, Alaska, USA: Getty Images

Red deer antlers that were used as chalk mining picks: Natural History Museum

Dr Chris Stringer with the skull of Cheddar Man: Michael Stephens/PA/Empics

Adrian Targett, Gough's Cave, Cheddar, Somerset: South West News Service

A reconstruction of Cheddar Man created by the University of Manchester: Natural History Museum

Chapter 4

Oat plant: © Klaus Hackenberg/zefa/Corbis

Archaeological dig: Corbis

Bone flute: Heritage Image Partnership/© British Museum

Lesser celandine: Mabel E Step in *Wayside and Woodland Blossoms*/Mary Evans Picture Library

Pottery bowl, about 3300-2700 BC: British Museum.

X-ray of the chest of a patient after recovery from pulmonary tuberculosis (TB): Science Photo Library

Milk pouring from bottle into glass: Masterfile

Imitation of a Sumerian plough: Dorling Kindersley

Stonehenge, Wiltshire, England: © Eyebyte/Alamy

Compliment card: Natural History Museum

Hadrian's Wall: Getty Images

Chapter 5

Penny Black Stamp, 1840: Mary Evans Picture Library

William Shakespeare by Martin Droeshout © Archivo Iconografico, S.A./Corbis

The Beatles, 1963: Redferns/Music Pictures

Christmas card, by Sir Henry Cole and by John Calcott Horsley: © V&A Images

Disc brooch, from Benevento, Campania, Anglo-Saxon, 7th century:
   © Ashmolean Museum, University of Oxford, UK/Bridgeman Art Library

Helmet, from the Sutton Hoo Ship Burial, Anglo-Saxon, (7th century): British
   Museum, London, UK/Bridgeman Art Library

Edward I (1239-1307) of England in February 1301: British Library, London,
   UK/Bridgeman Art Library

Anne Widdecombe: David Mansell/Camera Press

Chapter 6

The Ring of Brodgar standing stones Orkney Islands Scotland: © Robert Harding
   Picture Library Ltd/Alamy

Maes Howe, Orkney: © Adam Woolfitt/Corbis

Carved Viking Runes: © Homer Sykes/Corbis

Viking Longship: © Hulton-Deutsch Collection/Corbis

The Lewis Chessmen 1150-1175: © British Museum

Margaret of Denmark: Mary Evans Picture Library

The Burghead Bull, Pictish, 7th century AD: © British Museum

At an excavation for Viking artifacts in Dublin: © Ted Spiegel/Corbis

Viking on British shore circa 890: Douglas McCarthy/Mary Evans Picture Library

Hudson Bay Company trading post store:Time Life Pictures/Getty Images

The Bayeux Tapestry French School, (11th century): with special authorisation of
   the city of Bayeux/Bridgeman Art Library

Facsimile copy of The Domesday Book, 1085-86: Bridgeman Art Library

Chapter Seven

Extinct African hominids by Maurice Wilson: Natural History Museum

Bald man: Alamy

Bleadon Man's skull: Science and Society Picture Library

Jeremy Irons: Fabio Lovino/Contrasto/eyevine

Liz Hurley: Empics

Chapter Eight

Thorpeness sign, Suffolk: Alamy

Chipping Norton, Burford: Alamy

Kings Norton: Alamy

Much Hadham, Hertfordshire: britainonview/Rod Edwards

X and Y chromosomes: Getty Images

David Attenborough: Camera Press

Lancashire signpost and signs: Getty Images

Lady Elizabeth Noel Wriothesley by Sir Peter Lely: Petworth House, Sussex,
    UK/Bridgeman Art Library

Botallack Tin Mines, Cornwall, England: Roy Rainford/Robert Harding

Jeremy Paxman: Camera Press/Ian Lloyd

Duke of Edinburgh: Tim Graham/Getty Images

Czar Nicholas II with family: Getty Images

Epilogue

Portrait of a man looking serious: John Birdsall Social Issues Library

Bereaved Mother: Getty Images

Scottish fisherman: Getty Images

Portrait of an older woman smiling: John Birdsall Social Issues Library

Index

FACE OF BRITAIN